AIKIDO WEAPONS

AND PRINCIPLES

A JOURNEY BEYOND CHOREOGRAPHY

By

RICHARD J. SMALL

Aikido weapons - engaging the mind beyond choreography.

Preferably the reader will already have an existing knowledge of aikido.

Through the medium of story and analogy, the purpose of this book is to offer you an opportunity to think, and to think in a way that creates an awareness leading to sensory feeling. Though thinking destroys feeling, we often have to take that path in the beginning.

Be aware that intention and spirit are not quite the same as is normal everyday thinking, for that exists in the head alone.

Please don't take my word for any of it.
You should always test ideas out for yourself.

There will be omissions and mistakes too, if I await its perfection it will never be published.

I have expressed opinions based on my understanding at the time of writing, but in any case you should never follow blindly.

*Make a point of learning
from the experience of your own practise.*

There is not a week should go by without discovering something of interest. *Therefore always be interested.*

Also, your teacher may have already told you as eventually happens to all students in life,

'You are on your own in this journey.
You must therefore find your own way.'

Perhaps the contents of this book will illuminate the wilderness a little so you can more easily find a suitable path.

Question in your own mind if what you read makes sense to you, for you are the map maker of your own world.

You are your own destiny and if not,
who the hell is?

Richard J Small

www.goodshortstories.net

My thanks to all those who gave the gifts of learning and to those who might accept mine.

Want to read some good novels
or write a book yourself?
Go to www.goodnessmepublishing.co.uk

Contents.

Section 2. Technical and practical.

Section 3. Amusement only.

***

1.   The Sculptor.

"Remove from your practice that which it isn't and, like the master sculptor, you will be left with only that which it is."

"Like the master sculptor, you should be aware that there is always something even better hidden within."

2.   On teaching.

Teaching requires patience and humility as well as great skill. Teach others, don't just demonstrate how good you are. As we all learn in different ways, teach in different ways. Ideally the teacher will need ten times more knowledge than the student, as well as the skill to actually pass it on. Teaching is a great privilege and responsibility, for it can influence people's lives for good.

3.   Aikido. . . . just what are the principles?

Pay attention to; - correct angle, distance, timing and attitude.

Ensure; - weight underside, relaxation, concentration on one point (energy out), extension.

Nothing stands alone, everything is interconnected, however, we say the first principle is to escape the attack. . . which paradoxically we invite, then comes blending and connecting. In which order do they come? Shouldn't we have connected before the attack began? We take the attacker's balance. . . but do we, or do we lead them to an apparent place of safety, where they unknowingly give up their own balance.

There are the principles that relate to your interaction with the attacker during which you alter the circumstances of advantage to yourself.

Then there are principles that relate solely to your self, whether there is an attacker or not and which can and should be practised whether or not an attacker is present. Sound posture, balance and attitude. Correct connection throughout your own body and mind, your mind in the right place for the action. What you need from your mind is yet another deep paradox. How do you use your mind to do nothing, isn't using it actually doing something? How can you be 'out of your mind' yet still use it to extend Ki? I'm sure there are more questions I've as yet to discover.

There are principles for the body and those for the mind; is this something that can be understood but never explained? What do you think? It is what you think that matters, for it guides you in life.

***

4. Doorways, gates, portals.

On our way, (Do), through life, we pass by many doorways of opportunity. Some we do not see, some we see but do not stop, some we try but they do not open, some open but we enter not therein, and some we enter through. Beyond those doorways we entered, there may be an enlightenment, a discovery, an experience, which we may or may not recognise for what it is, for 'seeing is not seeing'.

Sometimes we try to return to a doorway having realised its worth but now it may not open for us. We are indeed fortunate if we are awake to the opportunities that unfold before us, as you may find yourself now.

Many times we awake when the path has long ago passed by that doorway ... even in that there is a lesson to be discovered. The goal is the path itself and not as we think, the destination, for there isn't one, we only think there is.

'Tomorrow does not exist.'

Our path is blessed if it travels through time in Ai Ki (harmony of Spirit). Keep your eyes on the path and what is on it. Eyes looking far into the distance mean none for the path.

Beware that the fog of thinking can obscure the doorways. Consider the paradox of, not thinking and yet all will be revealed.

Just like a rolling stone gathers no moss a moving mind gathers no thought. Keep the mind moving. Thought is not required, what is required is inspiration and intuition. Both of these will arrive uninvited when the thinking mind is quiet.

'Calm is always the key'.

***

5.   An interview with the author, Richard Small, back in July of 2017

Q. What inspired you to do aiki jo?

Training with weapons needs no mats, it is something you can practise alone or with a partner, you can practise in street clothes and footwear, anywhere you go, the forest, the beach, your home or garden - you can pick up any stick, broom handle, hoe, umbrella, walking stick, even a twig and enjoy your connection with the spirit of aikido. As a teacher moving to the area alone, it was an art that lent itself to teaching beginners who had neither equipment nor experience.

It is also an art within the reach of almost any person, regardless of their age and ability.

Q. What are the aims of martial arts?

Qualities possible from martial arts practice.
Perception; awareness; confidence; patience;
friendship; communication; adaptability; resilience;
loyalty; reflection; humility; perspective; compassion;
honesty; empathy; discipline, (both external and self);
humour; co-ordination, (of mind and body); flexibility;
intuition.

These are transferable skills
that will always serve you well in life.
They are freely yours for the having.

Aiki Jo can also be used as an exercise system,
training aspects of self defence, developing health
defence, improving confidence, body awareness, co-
ordination, social and self awareness, balance and
power, even engaging in a pathway to moving
meditation and finding the path on which your spirit
walks.

Weapons encourage your ki (spirit energy) to
extend beyond self.

Q. What plans do you have for the future?

I started a martial art when I was in my
twenties, probably for much the same reason as
anyone else. I sought a security from the
confrontations that often beset the minds of youths.

Martial arts are a great reality check for the Ego.
You suddenly discover that the art you have taken up
to defend yourself is full of people much more able
than you. You try harder to catch up, to improve

fitness, co-ordination and technical skills. Often, it is many years before the spiritual side of the art becomes apparent. The mind/body/spirit connection makes you more calm, centred, and peaceful; And yes, more powerful. Do not confuse strength with power. When you understand, 'Do nothing and everything is done,' then you have arrived at the gateway you seek. After more than forty years of training, I plan to keep looking and try and make what I understand, possible through my actions. Still a long way to go – but the journey remains ever more important than the destination.

***

6.   Remembering my teacher's lesson

A recollection from 1998 and my teacher's lesson. They were often carried out with short stories –

"the path there is and many seek it, the map there is and many hold it. As we progress, more of the map becomes clear. Sometimes a tree (a problem) will bar our way. If we detour then, we must remember why we did so, for if the tree is later removed, we must return to the old path.

> *The detour was not the true path,*
> *merely a convenience of the time.*

Eventually we will not seek the path nor will we ever know that we are on it, for then, we will *be* the path."

***

7.   Of Aikido and of leaves in Kefalonia.

(An analogy with aikido. . . but you're going to have to look for yourself!)

Early one fine summer's morning, when an Ionian Sun had just risen above the skyline of Mount Aenos and yet already bathed the garden in a fiery light, the student selected one of the brooms by the back door and headed left to a nearby leaf strewn path. Lesson one, be careful what you choose; that refers to both broom and path!

He knew there were lessons to be had in sweeping the path; lessons often more profound than we can imagine; perhaps one would show itself this day.

There are, of course, many paths, each with its own teachings; the one shown in the photo is not the path he chose to sweep; why might you think that it was? *Seeing is not seeing* and we are beset by illusion and inference in life. The answer will often be an opposite of that which you at first thought. Think on this, for it is a valuable principle to use in life. The uneven surface of the grey, crazy paved stones seemed to trap the fallen eucalyptus leaves that strewed the path. The brush he had inadvertently and unquestioningly chosen was a stiff bristled synthetic affair and he at first blamed it for its failings, indeed he blamed it for all failings, thinking that a wider, softer one would be much more effective. Was this the lesson? No, it seemed not, there surely must be more. Keeping the brush he had chosen but changing the direction of sweep soon had the reticent leaves shifted from their erstwhile homes.

Could this be the lesson. . . changing direction?

It was certainly one of sorts but surely he must look further, deeper. Perhaps using the brush was just practice for the Jo. Could it be that simple?

He began to move leaves from right to left so that he could more easily sweep a whole line of them over the edge into the wild oblivion that lay beyond the formalised garden. This wasn't a punishment for the leaves; they were going to be happier where he sent them. Most went willingly. His plan functioned reasonably well and the great majority were easily brushed away and dismissed from the perceived battlefield. It however left a few tenacious, conflict hardened beasts that denied his every move. Even on flat stones the elongated Eucalyptus leaves clung like limpets. The harder he brushed the more they resisted, looking up mockingly at his efforts, laughing, as if they knew the secrets and they could see that he did not. The more strength he added to the brush the closer it came to failing in itself, and he with it.

He paused, relaxed a little and instead tried the lightest touch with the brush and, there in the capitulating tumbling leaves, lay the answer. Use correct technique and never add power; concern yourself only with disrupting the leaves' stability, only engage in a direction which will prove useful. Then the leaves will cease to become opponents but become partners on the path. No energy was added to the weight of the leaf by pressing, instead the energy ran parallel to the ground and once the leaf was ungrounded it was at the brush's mercy . . . and none was given !

Sensei Anton in Gedan Gaeshi

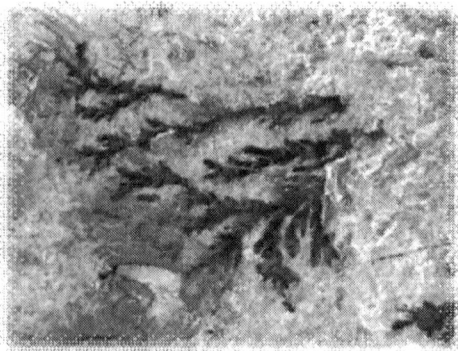

Another day arrived; another brush was chosen and before them, the same path, now fresh strewn with wind blown debris from the generous Eucalyptus that forever shared its leaves with the earth. The brush, new to him yet perhaps old to others, was softer. "This is much better," the student thought satisfyingly, "much better. . . no need for great pressure, this soft brush is working well." Each piece of stone was swept, each piece of stone was new, and each sweep of the brush was new. Perfection was sought with every action as if it was unique and all that existed; smooth, flowing, efficient and successful; then, on to the next stone and the process repeated in a manner as if it were the first time.

Suddenly a gift appeared before his eyes, there in the stones so carelessly swept before, he saw the signs of ancient life. . . fossilised plants and perhaps a promise of more to find. Now each stone was brushed more carefully, the student's awareness raised to what the moving leaves might uncover. What joy, what discovery might be behind every leaf on the path. . . the destination became the path itself. The routine of sweeping a path became a series of profound lessons. Brush, leaves, stones, the path and the student himself all took on new meaning.

When someone asks you to sweep their path, accept it as a gift and think on what I have written, for nothing will ever be as you think it is. Much, if not all of your world, is illusion, as may this be too.

***

8. Sweeping the temple floor.

In many an Aiki Dojo across the world, it is not an uncommon day break practice to sweep the surrounding yards and pathways. Why is it done? For the pride in your Dojo? To keep visitors feet clean for the tatami? So that the Sensei can exert power over you?

'Sweeping the Temple Floor'

Because the Sensei had years of path sweeping under his belt too? Let us consider our reasons. The early morning cleansing sweep is no different as dawn rises at Sensei Tony Sargeant's Koriana Dojo on Kefalonia. (Now closed) The change is not just for the path surface but for the sweeper; perhaps the sweeper becomes the swept.

Rising before 6.00am, students sweep the paths and courtyards of the Koriana Dojo in the warm dawn air; as they sweep pristinely onwards, nature acts as nature does and once more decorates the ground with fallen leaves and bougainvillea flowers behind them. What change there? ...the ground itself is still the same. . .only the leaves are new. The circle is endless. Perhaps in this we have a clue.

We may also, through our endeavours, recognise that which we can change and that which we cannot; another clue as to purpose.

So, why do we do it? Firstly, it is expected of you. There may be a penalty to pay should you arrive late. (Ah, is this another lesson here?) We learn to obey, both the Sensei and the rules but we also learn to share and to care. We work in harmony with others, avoiding sweeping our collected debris and troubles on to another's space. Blending our efforts in harmony we help those who struggle with the task and we accept help from those who give. (Any lessons there?)

You sweep for the sake of others, that their efforts and sufferings as they may be are not worsened by your own omissions or lack. You let no one down; a humble and humbling task has become an honourable achievement; a sense of this flows within you, you are a small step further down the path of Aiki, a small step, a small victory.

*Perhaps the 'why' and the 'how' of the matter
are inextricably entwined.*

Is the purpose only to have a clean path? No, it surely is not, for that is a destination that may never be reached. As ever, the path is the goal itself, the path you walk is your destination.

How should you sweep? Well that is up to you to discover. What should you think? That too is up to you, for it is your own individual path to follow. . . and your path to sweep. (An old proverb says, 'he who is carried to the temple gates will never know how far it was.')

I share with you here my own current and no doubt transient understanding which I encountered while sweeping such a path.

Time – it is always so hard to find the time, so we have to make the time, and the Dojo at dawn is when you make the time to sweep the path.

Sensitivity – applying the pressure on the brush and in a way that the flimsy dojo brush will not bend or break. (Believe me, they do, as someone I know quite well has broken three already!)

Sensitivity and patience – how to move the tiny leaves that grip the earth like a hundred kilo 9th Dan and yet simultaneously how to control the little round seeds that roll and scatter in all directions

Control – how to hold the brush and explore tsuki or gedan gaeshi; a chance to explore the inner connections of both body and mind in a peace of your own making; a chance to repeat the movement a thousand times yet with each movement of the brush to engage the beginner's mind.

Beginner's mind – the beginner's mind is ever in the 'now'. Each new sweep of the brush is a 'now' moment in which all is new yet all is changing. No preconceptions about the next sweep, no memories of the last one. . . unless you broke the brush. Think on this next time you practice in aiki.

Inner calm – as you begin to sweep, the thinking mind is active yet soon transforms to the intuitive state as the simplicity of your task leads you to a calmer state of mind.

Attacker or attacked ? perhaps the path is uke to your nage. . . or perhaps it is nage to your uke . . . or is it neither. . . and you are one. . .you decide.

So many lessons there are on the path, be attentive and they may show themselves.

***

9. A principle that weapon's practice supports.

Regardless of style, how often will you have heard the advice, 'extend', whether it be to extend ki or merely to reach out physically? When you extend ki there will always be an unintentional and often unrealised slight physical extension anyway; it is better to think of it in an energy way rather than extending only physically, for that can lead to tightening of muscles and locking of one's own joints.

If you observe any of the great masters their 'extension' is evident, it is clearly visible. Old film of O-Sensei shows his extension both energetically and physically. So let us presume this is an essential part of the art we follow.

How do you use your Aiki weapons? Do you extend your mind into the weapons? Do you reach out, keeping joints relaxed but open? Do you maintain good connection, not only between you and the Jo but with your arms and the rest of your body? Are you relaxed and yet focussed (concentrated) in your movements? Is the grip you have relaxed, connected and effective? Do you keep the Jo (weapon) in harmony with your body?

Explore an idea; Try any weapons move you know. . . preferably very slowly, and consider the relationship with yourself and the Jo at all times during the move.

Is your own action causing your joints to be stressed? A common example is in high Tsuki, if the hand is too far away from your body there is a tendency for the fingers to be wrenched open   ... aikido isn't meant to self inflict damage to your own body. Hands should always be able to retain a relaxed grip; this allows the shoulders to relax too. If it doesn't feel right then it probably isn't. Using the mind to extend Ki does not mean that any of your joints are locked nor your muscles tight. . . a controlled relaxation is the result. In the high tsuki mentioned earlier, the arm may be bent but there is a sense of opening and reaching out which gives it its power. . . it is truly connected and at one with the whole body. Extending Ki is an essence in weapons work and therefore can develop that principle into a habit that is available to you in all your aikido.

Sergei Stoliarov and Mark Allcock, Kefalonia

10. Ki, extension and relaxation equals power.

Ki . . . Imagination. . . belief gives birth to power . . . the energy can become a reality.

Extension with relaxation enables the body to unite as a whole, leading to power.

The power is in the joints – in the space between them. Just like the space in a wall is the gateway to another place. If you are familiar with the 'unbendable arm exercise' you will recognise this. The space between contains opposites which work in harmony to create a whole.

When relaxing you should feel a quiet, calm expansion in the joints, the mind is drawn to outside of the body rather than within and the sensation of weight on the body becomes lifted as the feeling of having joints disappears.

"In nothingness, there is everything".

***

11. Concern for teaching. . . my question answered.

"We never know what we give until it's been given, and then we may be the last to know if it did arrive in the way we thought it should."

Tony Sargeant Sensei

***

12.   Fear is the crossing place.

Find the balance between the defeat of your mistakes
and the inflation of your successes.
The middle way is calm and relaxed.
Fear of making mistakes creates a tension that
prevents you crossing to a better place.
Don't let thoughts take away feelings,
for it is they that might guide you all the better.

**

13   Why do we bow to O-Sensei ?

These are my own views, based upon the
teachings of others and my own experience. It's an
amalgamation of eastern and western culture but
which retains value for self and respect for others.

Bowing is a mark of respect in many cultures, so it follows that respect is primary. You might add other feelings too, gratitude or admiration for a start. Perhaps you only bow out of habit, because everyone else in the class does. It becomes just another thing you carry out before warm ups and the proper aikido you signed up to do. Perhaps you bow mindlessly, thoughtlessly, without feeling. Perhaps your bow is meaningful but travels only one way . . . 'what can O-Sensei do for me?'

I am of the opinion that to gain the most from your practice you are best bowing consciously, perhaps with a sense of both giving and of receiving. Strange as it may seem the act of kindness and its effects confer more power upon you than not. So in a way, kindness is unselfishly selfish.

Respect the mat and the dojo, respect your teacher and partner and respect is returned. This is a good lesson for everyday life and in part this too is one of the great benefits of training in the art.

Sometimes students clap their hands during the bowing sequence. It might well be said that you should only clap if there is a kamiza present. (The little wooden house where we might imagine the spirits dwell.) The clapping is supposedly to request that the spirits join you and help you in your quest. Once again that seems a one way street of, 'what's in it for me?'

There may be more than one reason for placing the hands together in 'prayer' position. Connecting hands in such a way connects left side of body with right side, making you naturally whole. It connects two major pressure points (nerve centres) in the palms together, one side being Yin and the other yang. It creates a balance of opposites with harmony.

I read recently that the first of two claps is to connect outwardly, to send out your spirit to connect with the universal and that the second clap is inviting the universal to come and join with you. You can try this for yourself, I'd almost make a bet that you will find it very difficult to experience either the out or the in whilst making the clap. It is easier when your mind is quiet and the body not active.

Whatever you chose to do and whatever your reasons you will still find it beneficial to have a purpose of good intent and to engage with it meaningfully. Keep vigilant for new learning.

There is more to Aikido than technique!

*If you ever think you have arrived,
then you have lost the path.*

Ken tai jo in Cambridge

14. Let wisdom be the hero for the day.

My soul didn't ask me to write this, it demanded it of me. The trouble is the language of the soul doesn't translate very well into English and there are some concepts that find no words in our language. However, I shall do my best, which is probably what you do too. . . or at least that's what we often say we do.

Poor old O-Sensei, he had such a noble dream to reconcile the world in peace through aikido. It might just be possible if we all tried harder for that goal. I am minded of a story about two birds discussing snow and its weight; one said, "Snow is so light, it weighs nothing, why I have seen it lifted in the wind." The other replied, "I think not friend, for I once watched snow landing on a mighty tree branch, snow flake after snow flake and the branch held strong . . . until just one single snowflake more landed and that branch was felled. . . just one more that's all."

The moral being perhaps that in life situations, we can be that tiny thing that finally tips the balance.

But I digress, the soul wants me to write of other things; to question why we might do aikido, what qualities do we seek. . . if at all, what teachers we might follow, who do we think should be practising aikido or not, more importantly; who or what do we aspire to, who to emulate, who to cast aside. Are they not all snowflakes? If none of this means anything to your own soul don't read any more, go and do something that you think is more important. It's your soul that matters and not the calculating, time constrained egoistic left side of your brain; you know the side that just looked at how many more lines there are to read, or the clock, or thought about a snack, or what's on TV. It's the side of the brain that will let you down one day when it decides it doesn't know the answer. . . an answer that your soul knew from birth but you don't listen.

When we are young, lots of not so old people actually look really old to us and we foolishly look down on them, seeing them as less able or defective in some way, that we of course are not. I learned a lesson many years ago for which I remain grateful. I had not been practising aikido that long but had risen to the dizzy heights of yellow belt. My teacher at the time, Sensei Aubrey Smith, had organised a workshop with a visiting teacher at our small dojo in Wellingbrough. I sat on a chair in the dojo along with another yellow belt, I think his name was Mick, a swimming instructor he was. We were waiting for a few more to turn up when this seemingly short and elderly chap came in and put a briefcase down on a chair before leaving the room again. Mick and I looked at each other, we were amazed that this little old chap (as we saw him from our twenty year old eyes) was going to attempt aikido. Didn't he realise it was a martial art and required youth and strength to perform. . . why, he was just wasting his time. Our Sensei entered the dojo and we lined up ready for the start; the visiting teacher entered and we were totally gob-smacked that it was the old chap we had written off before. He was a second Dan at the time and we know of him now as 8th Dan Sensei Pat Stratford. I was to meet Sensei Pat again when we travelled to his club in Coventry, where he hosted a course with Sensei Andre Noquet of France . . . another old man, (from our twenty year old eyes). Please realise that I write with affection and respect for these masters, past and present. I may not remember the techniques but I remember the men and the lessons I learned and I have gratitude for their unstinting devotion to the art and to the efforts they made to share it with others.

I also recall an elderly man who trained with us in Cambridge; it was annoying if I found that he was my partner because I couldn't throw him about and inflict my 'aikido' on him like with a younger 'proper' uke. How sad that we can practice an art about which we often understand nothing. It shouldn't have mattered about his age, it is not up to uke to develop our aikido but it is up to us; another valuable lesson from the 'has-beens' as we so foolishly think them.

O-Sensei was an old man, why don't we discount him too, or perhaps you have.

There are a few of these older chaps about and so often they have little publicity and fewer students, a handful at most. Many students want a dynamic teacher, a Bruce Lee type, not someone who looks like they live in an old people's home. They choose a teacher that fits their mind set and what they think they want from aikido; that too will change them with the changing years . . . if they keep going that is, for many will abandon the art when it no longer suits their ageing body. The art will never abandon us, it is we who are guilty of that deed. The older teacher probably has the answers to which the younger student hasn't even discovered the questions.

Whatever we do in life, much of it will have depended on the help of others. . . you'd be dead now if your parents hadn't fed and looked after you, you don't make your own clothes you probably don't gather your own food, you wouldn't be reading this if someone hadn't taken the time and trouble, to teach, to help and guide you. You think you did it all yourself? Then you suffer from another problem that martial arts should help you with. . . ego, let's make that **Ego**. O-Sensei wrote about taking the sword and cutting down the enemy. And where did he suggest we would meet this enemy? Inside, of course. What form did O-Sensei suggest this enemy would take? I'm not sure that he extrapolated on his suggestion but I would hazard a guess that it wasn't anything on the following list; loyalty, honour, integrity, gratitude, patience, endurance, tenacity, compassion, generosity, understanding, harmony, spirit, in fact harmony of spirit through our endeavours.

I nearly wrote some more there, but have deleted it as I realised it was not my soul but my thinking brain that wanted to say it and there is no place here for such thoughts.

I will close by thanking all my teachers whoever they were or are, in life or in death, some gem of wisdom has stayed with me from each and every one, I am grateful for all the efforts they made in the search of their art and their willingness to share it freely.

Let wisdom be the hero for the day.

***

15. Remembering and learning

We forget much, even some of the really important things, but because we still actively study the art, we come across new learning. Someone opens the gateway to what was hitherto hidden from view ... perhaps it is even our own gate that we kept closed until then. Armed with our new learning, old memories are triggered and we see the similarities for the first time. We have joined two more pieces of the great puzzle. Only by more study will we discover the other pieces, never close your mind to what might be.

Never give up the search.

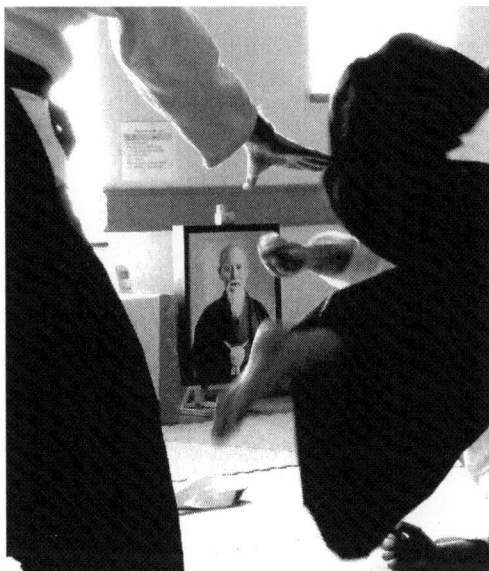

***

16. What's wrong with Aikido if you want it as street style self defence.

What's good about it if you want a spiritual path that aids your well being.

No mats - can't do - why not ... want to throw
Attitude ... winning - it's the attitude that is wrong - ego - shame

During half the class you are learning to be useless.

No old people - no children

I'm sure, just like I have, you have considered the stylised attacks we so often see in aikido training. You will probably have also noted that the typical street attack uses none of these attacks. Most street attacks will involve an arm reaching out, either to grab or to range-find or will involve a direct swinging punch to the side of the head. Even primitive man was aware of the effects of a blow to almost any area on the side of the human head.

Perhaps our aikido isn't preparing us for these attacks but developing transferable skills. Even so, the half hearted, probably won't hit you anyway, pre telegraphed and slow strikes that end with a dead stop and a long wait for the defensive move to occur might still provide useful training for nage. I suggest that it is counter productive training for uke. They are learning to telegraph moves, overbalance themselves, lose awareness, expect to fall over and expect to lose. Sometimes you see the uke prepare for the ukemi before nage has effected the technique. This is a wonderful example of blending and compliance but I suspect it is short changing the student for half of his training session . . . the half in which he is uke.

I think the attacker should be placed in a position where they realise they cannot win and that they will arrive there not knowing how it happened. Because what they do not know, they cannot counter. If you blend with then 'attack' your opponent they will feel your attack. Something more subtle exists ... it is aikido ... what are we doing ?

17. What's your opinion on relaxation in Aikido?

I'd like to share some thoughts and learn from those that might offer their own. I'll say a little more on interpreting the term relaxation later but, regardless of its manifestation.

> *'Relaxation can save your life;*
> *stress and panic can take it.'*

For example:-

Worry ... is paying a price that may never be asked.

Swimming, float when caught in a rip tide.

Confined space... trapped...a relaxed body is smaller.

Boxing.... No endurance without relaxation, no speed without it either.

Car crash... not suggesting you should drink and drive, but drunks nearly always walk away.

Breakfalls... relaxed, don't hold breath. Tension may be injurious.

Note how all the above bear a direct relationship to the all important point of contact. How you interact with it determines the success or not of the outcome. Does that not apply to our aikido?

Tension, too much want and resistance are surely enemies of good aikido.

Success comes from, not adding, but in giving something up, like a great sculptor removing the worthless to reveal the perfection beneath.

Even intention can create tension. The initiation of intent encourages the hidden muscles in your body to cooperate with that intent and subtly engages them. This tension is visible to highly experienced martial artists even though the person they observe may not be aware of it at all. This can be experienced in most if not all of Ki exercises. The relaxation we really want is a relaxed connectedness, no slack in joints and nothing you still have to connect, before moving.

So, if you are going to have intention at all, let it be the intention to connect the whole body without tension.

This brings us on to compliance or complicity in practise. How can you practise your art if the attacker goes along with every thing you do – even if your 'technique' is incorrect. If you apply a lock with force, are you not then becoming the attacker and therefore vulnerable to the skilled aikido practitioner. But of course they are not allowed to use it, because it is not their turn.

Should not the attack be as meaningful as a real one within the sensible limits of practise and the receiver lead the attack without force to a place where the attacker's power and balance are so weak that they succumb to the 'technique' without argument or even an understanding of how it happened. Using force gives the other person information on power and direction.

If you meet force with force then usually the strongest wins. As we know, this is not the principle we adopt in aikido, in fact we might advertise the art as one in which a small person can use the power of a larger more powerful adversary against them. At times this appears laughable but with real skill, probably more than most of us will ever find, it must be possible.

So, what do you think about complicity in practise, where the attacker might end up using the essential sensitivity and relaxation that should be the prerogative of the receiver.

The man we purport to follow
yet mostly seem to ignore.

Huw Collingbourne founder of

Hartland Aikido in North Devon says,

"My own view is that if you are true to the essence of aikido you must both take away the strength *and* (using balance and blending) make the technique work. 'Softness' is no excuse for ineffective technique. The technique must *always* work, no matter how soft your style may be. If your technique fails you must go away and re-think it, not (a) ask the uke to behave differently (as far as I am concerned the uke is always right and should never be blamed for a failed technique) or (b) make it work by adding in strength. It is the constant search for effectiveness without force that makes aikido a continuing challenge even for people like us who've been doing it most of our adult lives."

And from 'Takemusu Aikido'
A Martial Artist's Journey of Discovery in Aikido
A Personal Account and Technical Explanation
By Tony Sargeant – 6th Dan Aikikai

'I felt full of confidence and ready to show Sensei just how good I was and I was certain the compliments would come in abundance the moment he first used me as Uke. This was far removed from what actually happened. Saito Sensei was so delighted once he heard a person had come all the way from England just to train with him that I was given the best position in front of his teaching. After only one day I was in front on the mat holding his wrist and I knew I had him. I was grounded and his soft squidgy wrists seemed completely mine, I squeezed just that bit more and he very slightly staggered. I knew my ten years of hard training was paying off. The next second I was thrown as if I were a piece of scrunched up cigarette paper and as I looked up from the ground, wondering what had happened, Saito Sensei spoke to the class of Auckland University students with these words: *"Tony is the strongest man on this Tatami (mat). . . I feel sorry for him; if he does not lose his strength he will never find O-Sensei's aikido"*. From the moment he said "Tony is the strongest man on this mat' to "if he does not lose his strength" I went from bathing in great glory to feeling the size of a mouse.'

Such students go on to become masters of the art.
A title they will readily deny.

***

18. A great paradox to success .... I think.

Seeing what you desire in the pool of water, you reach in to make it yours. But when you pull it out it is no longer what you saw. Seeing and perspective can be illusions.

What you search for you must try hard to find, but in its finding, what you looked for will disappear. It will be there but you won't know it as the thing you first sought.

Though you must try hard to find, beware trying so hard that the trying overshadows the discovery that may come from a different way, a smarter trying.

What you look for may arrive when you look in the opposite direction and are able to see it for the first time. If this reads a bit weird, I'm not surprised, yet I am happy with my understanding so far of this paradox.

The more you think, the harder will be the discovery but one day in some unthinking moment, the answer will be yours.

A poor diet is not good for our health.

Just by knowing the words, can we call this true 'awareness'? Awareness of words alone cannot reach the depth of knowing which is truly worth seeking.

I once heard an interesting analogy about warehouses; if you want to build a home, then you visit the warehouse for your bricks and timbers. Now, what if the only materials collected are damaged. *'Sorry, we only have twisted timbers, some with woodworm, and crumbly broken bricks'.* What sort of home can you build with them?

Now, our subconscious is our own warehouse from which we take the materials to build our 'home' - the place in which the inner you lives.

Therefore be careful what you store in your warehouse, for upon this will depend the sort of 'home' in which you inhabit this earth.

So, for aikido. or any other art, put only the best materials into your warehouse, seek quality foundations - for they are your future; gather and build carefully with attention to detail, do not rush, build yourself a lovely home - for it is you and you alone that lives in it - until it falls down or there's a power failure!

Build well and you can live happier and longer.

19. Are you right in what you do?

Are you confident that you know what you are doing?

Is what you are doing what you actually thought it was or would be?

After 40 years practising the art, I am now hitting a confused patch. Not that what I have done didn't seem to work but I wonder now if it was real ai ki do. Was it really a harmony of spirit that I had? Did I inflict my aikido on others? Did I use my mind enough? Did I co-ordinate my whole body and mind enough? Was my desire to win too much? Should I have been more sensitive to the physical attack and more empathetic with the mind of the attacker? Should I even have considered it an attack and not a 'gift'. . . does this in itself contravene the spiritual ethic of aikido? I am no longer sure about these things but continue to look forward to finding out.

We often tell others, 'I do aikido', but do we really? What is real aikido, what was O-Sensei's discovery all about?

*'The journey is everything and for each of us
there is only one destination;
it's how we make our way there that matters.'*

Is the path itself the destination?
Even O-Sensei would tell you that he had yet to arrive at a destination, where all was known.

The path is the destination.

***

The late Tim Buswell Sensei with tachi dori

***

Morihei Ueshiba

If your heart is large enough to envelop your adversaries, you can see right through them and avoid their attacks. And once you envelop them, you will be able to guide them along the path indicated to you by heaven and earth.

***

20. Takemusu – the truce in war.

No doubt like many oriental words, the meaning of *'takemusu'* is liable to interpretation and the singularity of the word itself belies the volume of meaning it carries. In fact to those who know the kanji,

It is debatable if the word 'musu' is correct, however, semantics and Chinese origins to pronunciation aside, this is what O-Sensei called it. That alone should be good enough for us if we are willing to understand what he was prepared to share.

The heart of it is, Takemusu relates to the spontaneous creation of technique during a moment of harmonisation between attacker and defender. (Possibly even the use of the word defender may be too strong. The act during the takemusu moment is natural, peaceful, effortless yet unstoppable, to use the word 'defend' creates an impression of more overt effort and an imposing action.) We know by now that words are an imperfect tool and that only the foolish will take them at face value.

> *'The wise hear one word,*
> *but understand two,'*
> *- An old saying of some merit.*

Let us take the analogy of war. One country looks at another with which it has grievance or designs and if it thinks it has the power to overcome that country it might attack using its military force. But supposing the attacked country has skills, culture, weaponry or whatever, that stops the attacker's advance. There is a moment when the attacking country realises their mistake and seeks a truce. At this point two conflicting views come together as one view – that of the truce itself. Two opposing forces temporarily live together in harmony and terms are settled in favour of the country which was attacked. Remember the attackers have realised their efforts are to no avail, they have no hope of succeeding. If the country which was attacked negotiates a peaceful settlement without causing great suffering to the would-be assailants then the attacker can accept defeat. Should the winning side impose draconian reparations upon the loser then they have become the attacker and as history has always shown a vengeful continuation of repeated wars is the result.

I think that the truce in war, with all its realisations during a short period of non confrontation, is much like the Takemusu moment. It must carry honourable principles in order to have a lasting legacy.

Further to this, I think takemusu is more than just a moment in time. It is a moment in time that embodies the trained principles of your aikido and the spirit that was invoked by our founder.

In the execution (unfortunate word) of our aikido, mind must connect with body and yet being 'in the body' is more powerful than 'being in the mind'. We need to be balanced or our own consciousness is restricted, our 'inner' must be in accord with our 'outer' if our power is to manifest itself. In the takemusu moment, do not exert yourself in a way that you feel your own power, because if you can, then you are becoming the attacker again.

Your attacker must not be able to understand your power, only know it exists.

The attacker (or Uke, partner etc in aikido training) should reach a point where they realise it is futile to resist, in fact there is no desire to resist as no direct force is felt. With their balance taken they are lost and will fall. It is unnecessary to add force to their fall . . . it is their turn next, just like in the history of wars. So it is not just down to correct technique but the timing, manner and judgemental free attitude of the aikidoka that allows the takemusu event to be successful . . . physically and spiritually. It is almost an act of kindness in the face of the enemy, and

'one cannot defend oneself against kindness.'

On a personal note here, I have never been one of those brave ukes, but when my teacher threw me in Koshi nage I was happy to go with it. There was no force applied that I could resist and therefore to flow over the hips and to the mat seemed like the most desirable direction to go. Compare with some people who grab your arms and physically try and wrench you over, using an arm to flip your legs and perhaps giving a quick hip lift to ensure maximum effect. Once you feel the physical or known power of the thrower then you can resist, because you understand what they are doing, you know how to stop them. And the war continues. This is not aikido and certainly is missing the magic of takemusu which is effortless, kindly and superbly effective.

The truce leads to a peace with honour.

***

21. O-Sensei's poems, what do they mean to you?

I've chosen one verse from many; can it have meaning for you, a meaning that possibly is only for you. It is often the way, for to each of us the very same something can appear quite different.

> "Standing amidst heaven and earth
> Connected to all things with ki
> My mind is set
> On the path of echoing all things."
> *Morihei Ueshiba*

My interpretation is firstly that of an awareness that it is Earth that holds me up, (if, in your mind, you stand not on the earth but let the earth push upwards, strangely you will feel lighter) and an indefinable concept of some on high celestial heaven, essentially a place in your mind that is above you. (Might just be a concept created from extending consciousness beyond self and manifesting a sense of connection with the top of your head, the crown chakra or celestial gate).

Much of this 'mind work' is about creating mechanisms that in turn allow you to experience feelings that would otherwise be difficult to ever find

O-Sensei suggests 'standing amidst', so we can imagine heaven and earth as two separate entities and place ourselves between them. We then become the connection and the bridge between heaven and earth. (You may feel a slight and involuntary elongation in your spine when you do this. Opening spaces within the body is a way of becoming one with the spaces in the universe – for they are the same).

O-Sensei continues; 'connecting with Ki': imagine now your own consciousness, aura, Ki, life force, what ever you wish to call it, expanding in all directions, reaching out and as it does so touching the energies of everything around you . . . and as far out into the cosmos as you like, for your imagination is boundless.

The 'echo of all things' is merely your awareness that your own 'Ki' has touched and recognised the oneness in all it touches.

Well, for what it's worth, this is my interpretation at my current understanding. Perhaps if O-Sensei was here and I could understand him he might say, 'total cobblers' or perhaps 'not bad, keep looking'.

We will never know . . . or will we?

***

22. Do you want to know a Secret?

The founder is known as the great teacher, but I ask you, 'Do you know anyone, living or dead that reached the same level as O-Sensei? So, if he was the great teacher, why, despite commitment, techniques and principles, couldn't anyone else reach his level?

What he knew, at an esoteric level, he could not teach. Paradoxically it may have been the very mastery of his art itself that prevented him doing so.

If the secret is embedded in another person's own ability, how can it ever be yours?

Many believe that O-Sensei was the benevolent guardian of the great secrets by which means he achieved what he did. In fact, he tried his best to share them but often left his students puzzled. Many follow in his footsteps hoping that they too will find this illusive 'magic'. Is it a path to within self or to somewhere far beyond? How much of it is physicality, how much, the application of mind. How much is of the spirit?

How readily we use the words *harmony of spirit* to describe our art but do we really understand what spirit is? Without knowing what it is, how can we then find harmony? Are we tripped up by the invisible? Is finding spirit one of the true secrets?

*We might think, 'I know what spirit is,'
until we are asked to explain.*

The feelings you experience on gaining lesser secrets can still be quite euphoric, as if you were the only one. Even if millions had known this before you, it still feels like your discovery because, in part, it is just that. How many times has someone confided in you their great secret and you thought, 'I knew that already but hadn't made the connection.'

"There are secrets, then there are secrets that you are told, but they remain secrets because you don't understand them." *Tim Buswell in 2009*

The implication of a secret is that it is something being withheld from you by another, yet all unknowns are secrets and some unknowns will stay that way for eternity.

Peter R, also 2009, had sought the secrets for and by his self, he was invincible, finding his freedom had led him to places where energy became visible to him, even the strongest man present could not hold him; he was at peace with who he was and where he was. His freedom to experiment, study and practise without constraint led him to understand what others see as secrets. So, although we need a teacher, it can be the shadow of that same teacher that shackles you to certitude and prevents your own discoveries. You can never know his secret; you can only find your own.

Consider then, there is a secret, a true secret that is beyond ordinary human understanding. We even know what it is - it is something which cannot be taught, nor explained in words. As O-Sensei said,

"The Gods will not allow it."

"Inward truths and mysteries are inevitably secret for those, who lack the faculty to perceive them."

W. Wilmshurst.

Become calm, become quieter, and all that was always known to you will be revealed, and when it is, you will never explain it, for such words do not exist in the thinking world. Hence the old saying,

"He who speaks does not know,
he who knows does not speak."

A true secret is exactly that … subtle, powerful and indescribable.

"We sit around in a ring and suppose. But the secret sits in the middle and knows."
Robert Frost

Seek peace in the world and discover only illusion, for peace can only reside in those who walk that path.

***

23.   Aikido ... martial art ?

It is said,

'We can only ever hear
what our understanding allows us to hear.'

So how deep goes our understanding? Is aikido a martial art? In fact, what is a martial art? Is aikido an effective self defence against street crime? Are we truly honest when we examine our abilities and when we teach students? Do we examine deeply enough our understanding of the art we follow, or even at all? Do we visit other clubs and styles, moving out of our comfort zone, or do we think we have all the answers we need?

There are those who, though advancing well in aikido, decide that there is more to learn from somewhere or something else and they explore Cheng hsin, Systema, tai chi, or other arts, even yoga. What is it that makes them look elsewhere? From my observations, they usually find what they were seeking and what was evidently missing from their aikido journey. Often those other groups help and support each other better than we do in the so called aikido 'community'.

There are also those in the world that criticise us for calling our art 'self defence' and they say what we do is more akin in nature to the tea ceremony. Do they have a point?

Shouldn't we be more resistant to the trend of insularity and being competitive between styles, organisations and clubs? Why allow the 'others' to become the enemy in an art that seeks harmony? Is this really what O-Sensei sought? Yet we say we follow him and do this in his name?

Profound but so true is an old Chinese saying,

'Seeing is never seeing'.

Couldn't we work together more and help each other promote the art of aikido.

Aikido offers us:- An exercise system, training in aspects of self defence, developing health defence, improving confidence, body awareness, mind body co-ordination, social and self awareness, balance and power, spiritual advancement and even engagement in a pathway to moving meditation and above all a sense of peace.

"Aikido is not a technique to fight with or defeat the enemy. It is the way to reconcile the world and make human beings one family." Morihei Ueshiba, Founder of Aikido.

Also. . .

". . . comparisons of O-Sensei's sword work with classical sword schools are completely beside the point as his intention was **not to impart battlefield techniques but to show how divine energy channels**

**through the human body, the space around it, and
all throughout the Universe**."
From the Aikido Journal Newsletter, March 17, 2015

Such arts are mechanisms to improve life, yours!
Learning from the experience of your own practise,
question in your own mind if what you read and see
makes sense to you; for

> *you are the map maker of your own world,*
> *you are your own destiny.*

***

24.   Aikido and cross training.

Stick your ego in the cupboard and go and visit
another club, another teacher, even another art and
find out if they have something to which you were
previously blind. How arrogant are we if we look
down on others of lower rank and think, "they have
nothing to teach me." Go and find out, and be
prepared for a shock.

I cannot help feeling that O-Sensei, who none of us
are ever likely to emulate, found his answers from
diverse sources, dare I say, even from his farming
practises, never mind martial training. Yet many of us
think to find our own answers by aikido alone. True,
we follow our own way in life but is your aikido the
real thing? Can you make it work? Indeed, is that last
question indicative of a non aiki attitude in itself?

We may be strong, capable and very good at what we
do and though it may not be correct, time and
practise has made us effective despite any defect. It's
even worse if we never train with other styles or clubs
(or even other arts). Safe and stuck in our comfort

zone we deny ourselves the opportunity to grow. O-Sensei never stopped studying and exploring the mind body connection yet how body aware are we?

Will aikido give us conscious body awareness? If we don't let rank get in the way, a visit to another teacher may well bring a discovery to our advantage. But that challenges our sense of accomplishment, it rattles at the cage of our comfort zone.

After some 40 years of training, I am now more amazed at what I *cannot* do than what I *can* do.

I recently joined a large number of teachers from across the world at an all embracing seminar of aikido in Burwell, Cambs. An event promoted by Quentin Cooke for Aiki Extensions. I witnessed how a beginner, with only one lesson behind them, using true principles was more effective than I was with all my years of techniques.

I had become a prisoner of what I knew. Freedom sometimes presents a more challenging environment.

I'm not going to rabbit on about this but as older age approaches I have less fear about being open with my words. Many of us have forgotten what aikido really is and some of us never even knew in the first place.

At the very least, think on that for a moment or two.

The Chinese have a saying,

> *"Don't just accept – go see."*

25. Martial arts compared with dangerous occupations – comparing principles.

Maintain a safe and guarded posture, regardless of it being visible to others.

Develop all around awareness and sensitivity to any advancing danger.

Your intuition improves and a sixth sense develops about potential dangers.

Remain calm and focussed throughout.

Be adaptable and react intelligently to change.

Train well and often.

Promote the will to serve others.

Stand resolutely between others and danger.

Develop trust and respect, for they are reciprocal.

Convey only meaningful information.

Practise realistically and for any situation.

Train your spirit as well as your body.

Develop self discipline.

The quality of your actions and deeds become more important than the façade of ego.

At the core you find an empathy with others, a shared sense of brother/sisterhood regardless of creed, colour or nationality.

Aspire to being better, in your actions as well as within self. A good reputation must be earned.

Cultivate a deeper and ultimately beneficial appreciation of responsibility for your own actions. Consequences become a reality in your life.

With luck, you live through it all and the very act of living through it becomes reward in itself.

Techniques and consequences may vary but the principles, the real essence of each activity are likely the same. Facing up to risks to your health in any form raises your awareness to the value of life itself.

Wouldn't you agree?

***

26.   Choosing a way to train with weapons in line with the principles.

Based on my many years of training in the Aiki weapons of Saito Sensei from my own teacher Sensei Tony Sargeant, many years of tai chi practise and some very useful insights into Ki Aikido from Sensei Huw Collingbourne, I'd like to share some thoughts on training with weapons.

The Iwama style weapons training has given a foundation of techniques and applications. Their purpose is to change the body, express and extend spirit and develop skills in timing and distance. Tai chi has brought a philosophy and a set of principles that sit in harmony with my idea of aikido. The symbol we so often associate with tai chi represents opposites that abide in harmony not in conflict. The symbol has no beginning and no end; there are no straight lines and no breaks. The principles of Ki aikido, difficult to master as they are, offer abilities that seem at times, akin to magic. *(Essential though that you find the right teacher, the magician.)*

Would you agree that aikido requires sensitivity, connectivity and relaxation of the right kind, to effect the desired result on your training partner? Are Aiki principles generally counter intuitive to the human condition, which note, is also its greatest asset?

Training with weapons is an interesting and useful way to develop the harmony necessary for aikido and can help find the effortless power exhibited by some of the great past masters.

Only the receiver experiences the force but is unable to identify clearly where it came from, rendering them unable to make a counter.

How often have you heard expressions like, 'accept the gift,' 'please come past,' 'care for the attacker,' 'respect the partner's ki,'? All these expressions are there to take your mind away from the point of contact and allow your whole being to engage in the movement without tension and in a harmonious manner that leads to an inability to harm or control you.

Success for you, is not over them,
but over yourself.

If aikido requires sensitivity and leading the attacker to where they are willing to go – not where you force them to go against their will – then to exert unnecessary force will be counter to aikido principles. Any force the attacker feels, not in line with their own, will provide them with information to use against you.

Like it or not, weapons training was a big part of O-Sensei's practise and the development of his art and his own amazing skills.

If harmony is required in taijutsu then it must be also found in weapons or bukiwaza.

Taking the Jo or short staff as our example, it should be possible to make all the suburi and kata with the lightest of grip and to experience the moment without any effort except intention. Whether you wish to hold stronger is up to you and circumstances. But, if you can perform katate toma uchi (suburi number 12) with only a light thumb and finger grip, then you must have been in harmony with the Jo. Both you and the Jo travelled on a mutually agreeable path. The sort of harmony that you need in taijutsu and for what I now believe is the essence of aikido. The passive overcomes the strong because it needs to find the right path. Yin overcomes yang

All of your moves with weapons should take the path that is agreeable to the weapon. There are certain directions, almost exclusively along the length of the weapon, that provide that effortless path to aiki.

The weapon is not used to block but to blend, connect and neutralise and your own movement should be at one with that blend.

'Never have conflict at the point of contact',

is the prevailing principle here.

If you can't do it with the Jo, then perhaps you'll struggle to achieve it empty handed.

A harsh grip on the Jo can only slow and restrict your movements and possibly worse still, encourage you to make the Jo travel where you wish – right or wrong. Lighter grip more sensitivity, more harmony, better feeling.

It's the body and not the arms, that makes the move whole, and in doing so, will affect the training partner in the same way too i.e. through their whole body.

I neither know nor claim that this view is right but it represents my current belief based on the feelings I have during training.

Perhaps you might find it worth a try.

27. A Warrior's Journey?

I have to say that it's somewhat of an embarrassing title to me, and that in itself unveils one of my own long struggles in life. However, I tell myself that this story is born not of reality but of dreams and that in itself makes it easier to write. The enemy within is real enough, the internal enemies of ego and greed, of doubt, embarrassment, fear of rejection and humiliation. These are enemies that transcend race, creed, age, gender or ability, we are all equally at their mercy; a mercy seldom if ever given and never offered. It's been a long journey during which time of travelling I have often been tested and so often defeated, sometimes without realisation, so subtle is the enemy.

The one I've followed for 40 years now, had some ideas on this . . .

The penetrating brilliance of a sword wielded by a follower of the Way strikes at the evil enemy lurking deep within - one's own body and soul.
        Morihei Ueshiba

I woke early that Spring morning and gathered my belongings for the journey to yet another battlefield, for we always think it is some place else; yet unknowing, we carry it with us every where we go. Spare clothes, uniform and weapons were duly packed in my vehicle and the day felt good.

The day was good and I felt good, even if a little aged and with the odd pain in my hands – I considered at some depth what it might be and how long it might last. However, in general, it was a good day on which to set off to fight my 'war', a war I live in hopes of winning one day. By win, I mean, to find peace within. There is no anger or sense of revenge, no hatred or angst – for they too are our enemy within. It will often be they that choose the field upon which you will metaphorically do or die.

"I count him braver who overcomes his desires, than him who conquers his enemies; for the hardest victory is self."   Aristotle

Unusually the Sun is shining, if you live on the UK west coast you will know what I mean! The first part of the journey is without incident – all is peaceful – the world at large may be gripped in conflict but inside my car it was at peace. It's the only peace we can ever experience – our own.

The transport cafe was full of good natured drivers having their rest breaks. I ordered the large breakfast minus the beans and toast. Despite then being an advocate of the Palaeolithic diet, I accepted the fried potatoes.

There was no conflict between me and the potatoes. Though they were not on my 'list', in my heart they were not the enemy – not today. The motorways too were more peaceful this day; we all drove in harmony, all going the same way. (It helps, doesn't it?) The odd poor soul did cut across my path to take an exit for which they had prepared badly . . . or perhaps cleverly! I have to confess a curse did pass my lips, a pointless gesture as you will know yourself and it served only to damage me not them. My stress level was elevated, my immune system lowered and a few minutes of my life that could have been contented were otherwise made distraught.

The enemy within is a skilled and often smiling assassin, striking when the innocent is least ready.

The radio was tuned in to a pleasing programme, a gentle speaking man talked of quiet heroism in war; his chosen music was Amazing Grace with the band of the Scots Guards and Waltzing Matilda sung by a powerful and emotive Australian woman. Both were poignant and stirring music, as traditionally befits 'warriors' setting out to do battle.

I was travelling to meet with like minded colleagues, fellow warriors of the way.

They would be gathering in a harmony and friendship that can only be born of facing a common struggle. Each must fight their own battle but each would be bounded by others seeking the same success – comrades all.

United in a moment of peace, the uniformed warriors of the way with bright white gi and pressed black hakama, weapons ready but dormant by their sides, bow reverently to the founder's image and prevailing spirit. This is a brief encounter with real peace, humility and intention, this moment when they all bow together. Our leader stands before us, exalting us to do our best and to do only good in our efforts to defeat the enemy (within).

This was not a beginning, nor was it an end for it

would often appear that our journey has neither.

The experienced warrior shares hard won knowledge to keep others safe, because at some time and for some reason they felt those others needed to know. But perhaps others do not need to know; perhaps they don't want to know.

And so our warrior finds yet another battle, the one that requires coming to terms with it being their journey and theirs alone.

In any event, regardless of our ambitions, our glorious victories or shameful defeats we must make the most of our days on the path.

"The waving of the summer grass is all that remains of the dreams and ambitions of long dead warriors.

Japanese poet, Basho
***

28. Are you prepared?

When facing your partner in preparation for practise you should already have been in a state of awareness long before.

If you have to prepare
then you were never ready

However, in being ready, do not tense or give away your readiness to the attacker.

Your kens should not touch prior to the practise itself, for had they touched one of you should have taken the energy and entered.

The fact that kens touch and no action ensues is an

indicator that neither partners were truly ready. How often might you have heard the click clack of ken against ken ... sometimes even followed by a knowing embarrassment and apology ... when the teacher calls out, 'First kumitachi, three times and change.'

***

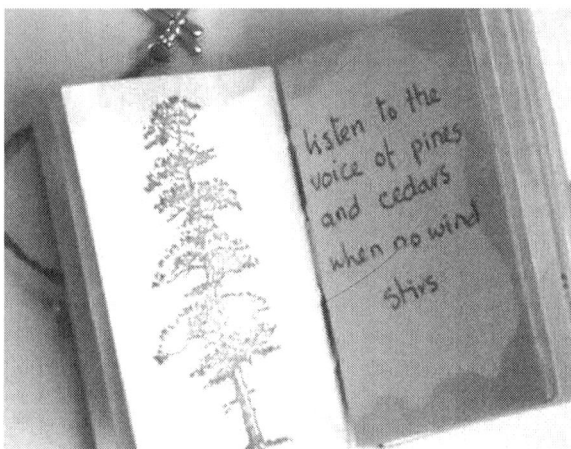

It is said that the faintest pencil is more powerful than the greatest mind.

***

29. Can this be the 'magic' in Aikido?

It's a little known but natural phenomenon called the *'ideomotor effect'* and has been written about before with regard to aikido, particularly in relationship to ki power. Simply put, muscles in the body join in with a person's will or belief without informing that same person they have done so. The person will be unaware that the muscles engaged, in fact they might even argue that they were relaxed at the time – they will not be aware of the underlying muscle involvement.

I've added a drawing of a tai chi posture (single whip) but it is only the knees I ask you to consider. I think we can agree that the knees are bent and therefore 'closing'.

If this were so then the strain would be enormous, but the practitioner would probably say that they felt no such strain and might even go on to say that they were comfortable and relaxed in this posture. Take a break from reading and try it for yourself if you wish. (No liability taken by the author!)

This is what I think she is doing; this is my understanding . . . as the knees bend and begin closure, her mind is doing the opposite, it is telling the knees to open. This in turn will trigger the *ideomotor effect* and bring muscles into play which balance the posture – balanced = no strain. We tend to think, the mind is doing it, but the mind is triggering muscles to act on our behalf without us knowingly engaging them.

This is one of the reasons we should at least look at other styles of aikido. Take Ki aikido or at least Koichi Tohei's view on it. There may be many teachers out there who do not commonly practise 'ki exercises', perhaps don't even know about them!

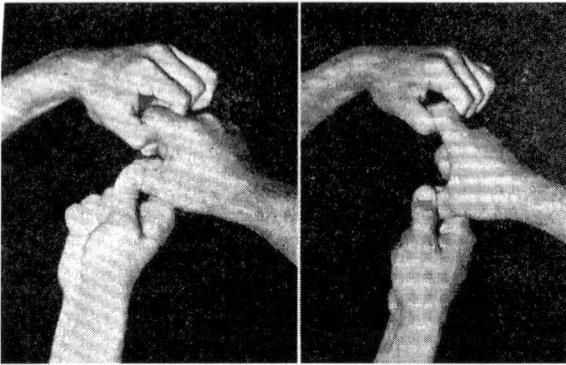

Here I've taken a picture from *Aikido in Daily Life,* showing thumb and finger held together, once by physical and known strength and the other relaxed but using mind power. The object of the exercise is to see which remains intact after a partner tries to pull them apart. By imagining/believing that the fingers make an iron ring they prove the most powerful. Power without effort.

How do you think the 'unbendable arm' exercise works? We never really question it, because it is the magic ingredient 'ki' isn't it? Well perhaps it is in a way. The better your mind is trained in channelling belief the better, the more relaxed your muscles, the easier energy can flow. Success in the practice breeds more belief and therefore greater success . . . but we continue to feel no physical feed back – in fact we feel even less. The big guy falls over and you wonder why he did, as you hadn't put any physical effort into the technique yet.

What about the age old story of the woman who lifts a car to save a child, yet afterwards cannot explain how. In such a case, instinctive and long hidden nature kicks in, maternal instinct, adrenalin and unity of mind, body and spirit combine with an unbreakable intent to achieve – simple as that. That's why we can't do it in ordinary life – because of how we are educated to grow up (eg, 'sit up straight!), nothing is connected up properly and our mind interferes with our true ability and causes doubt to act against our hidden powers. Don't do it, but you could go outside and try and lift your car now . . . doubt has already defeated you as you walk to the door. The martial arts are a pathway to change some of that.

The *ideomotor effect* also throws light on how another person can detect your intentions. Hiding what you intend to do requires some skill and practise. Remember, almost imperceptible muscle movements will occur the moment you create mind intent. Ever wondered why some people have 'seen' your attack coming so early that your attack has to follow and try and catch up – leading to your downfall? (Boxers can avoid punches that are so fast they shouldn't be able to – they have read the signals that precede the physical action). Highly skilled martial artists see these minuscule indications of intent, perhaps not consciously but at a deeper level they themselves cannot explain.

Ki exercises are one way to enhance your natural abilities. Call it what you like, even magic if you will, but it does exist and can be trained.

In conclusion;
Ki, extension and relaxation = power.
Ki – imagination – belief gives birth to power – the energy can become a reality.

Like in the tai chi practitioner's knees or the finger joints in Tohei's exercise, the joints are open, relaxed – it is the space between that allows the 'magic' to travel.

"In nothingness, there is everything."
You just need to ask your mind to take you there !

It's only my opinion . . . but I'm happy with it . . . so far !

***

O-Sensei: "In aikido, there is absolutely no attack. To attack means that the spirit has already lost. We adhere to the principle of absolute non-resistance, that is to say, we do not oppose the attacker. Thus, there is no opponent in aikido. The victory in aikido is *masakatsu agatsu* (correct victory, self-victory); since you win over everything in accordance with the mission of heaven, you possess absolute strength

***

30. More on relaxation - because It's probably not quite what you think it is.
Relaxation allows extension of the body and opening the joints.

Relaxation enables energy to flow and there is more 'mind' to it than we often think or use. It is less 'willpower' but more a subtle imagination or belief that is required. Willpower can create its own tensions and blocks.

A relaxed body is a united body and therefore has more power.

It is well said,

"where intention goes, energy flows",

but examine carefully the possible differences between where your energy goes and where your intention goes. Intention may be one directional (put simply) but energy may be expanding in all directions. The Chinese express it as Ba Men or eight gates, each of them opening in a different direction. Open them all.

Your imagination or belief for want of better description can also lead your energy or ki in other directions too, like spirals and circles and at some distance from your body.

***

"In true Budo there are no opponents –
seek to be one with all things."

***

31. Once upon a time in Kefalonia.

I watched Sensei Sargeant demonstrate different levels of understanding and speak of his discoveries. As I watched and listened the sense and truth of it was apparent, but I am unable to express it in words – it is simply a personal journey of discovery to be found in our own time and place ... and if we want to. A bit like a holiday snap of a beach or a tree, they mean little to anyone else ... other than those who have been there . At a certain level the practice of jo kata can almost seem like a more expressive version of counting prayer beads.

So, as my porridge cools and the island of Kefalonia warms in the Sun, I conclude that the Jo in all its forms is merely a companion to you on your path, the path, which like the kata, remains the same – a spiritual path – a journey of the higher self with the rest of you joining in as required .... if not then perhaps the path and Jo are not for you.

***

Section 2. Technical and practical section.

Boken for precision, Jo for flowing, the essence of each, inherent in the body and spirit of one who walks the path of aikido - way of harmony of spirit.

***

32. Jo description and advice

The Jo is a short staff, good ones made of Japanese Oak, its length varies with the user (from the ground to just under the armpit). Because of its length and the opportunity to use both ends, it can be used in carrying out techniques from Bo (long staff), sword and spear. It is evident in each case which weapon is being represented by the jo. Eg 22 jo kata fits spear.

Using the Jo involves relaxed postures and movements except for the moment of impact.

Being relaxed allows quicker movement, more whole body co-ordination and a degree of flexibility should the need arise to change direction.

The founder had three parts to his art called aikido:

1. Body techniques
2. The Ken, a wooden sword
3. The Jo, a wooden staff

They were used to achieve simple understanding. Saito Sensei (9th Dan) said 'when you use the weapons' think of body movements; when you use body movements think of the weapons.

***

33. When practising ken variations, (henka), here shown is a henka from the first kumitachi.

Make sure you keep your thumb and fingers in a safe place ....if you want to keep them anyway.

***

34. The basics of the Aiki Ken

The basics of the Aiki Ken are centered on the suburi and kumitachi. Familiarity with these fundamentals leads to an ability to acquire more advanced skills such as tachidori or "sword taking" techniques

Look straight ahead.

Don't open the front foot too far when changing posture as it will detrimentally effect hip movement on strike. (Some might say **only** use hips)

Narrow posture, as if walking a bridge parapet.

Pelvic tilt needs to be understood fully to make it effective and safe. (Easily possible to exagerate the movement and cause harm.)

Leading foot lands toes first, heel lands with end of boken cut.

Suburi is mind of no mind, do not think 'cut' but seek perfection of movement, complete peace and harmony with body and spirit.

Elbows not wider than shoulders.

35. Morihiro Saito Sensei: Aikido is generally believed to represent circular movements. Contrary to such belief, however, aikido, in its true KI form, is a fierce art piercing straight through the centre of the opposition.

Sensei Tony Sargeant 6th Dan
on a teaching point in the 5th suburi.

***

36. Furuya Sensei on Swordsmanship:

Letting go of the idea of "sword" and the idea of "action" is the meaning behind "willow in the gentle breeze." When the slight summer breeze blows, does the willow follow the "nature of the willow," or does it follow the "nature of the breeze?" Please think about this - in this lies the essence of sword technique.

***

37.   Using Jo or Ken.

Explore the value of weapons practice in improving posture, balance, timing and distance in aikido practice.

Explore one or two examples of internal power that lead to a centred sense of peace in the practitioner.

Explore the value of non conflict with the point of contact – e.g. deflect a powerful Jo thrust with the lightest of grip.

The value of 'opposites'.

This is principle based teaching and not just choreography.

Principles should be a constant even if politics, egos, opinions and learning are not.

We train slowly and purposefully in order that our bodies can inform our minds about what feels correct or not ...... and change what is asked.

***

"Your most dangerous opponents are fear, anger, confusion, doubt and despair."

***

38. Observation of posture.

Mark Allcock Sensei,
founder of Wellsprings Aikido Club.

Observe:- Hips engaged. Eyes engaged. Body centred.
Joints aligned. Expanding energy. Circles and
spirals. Connectedness. Martial. Awareness.
Preparedness. Spirit. Movement in stillness.
A worthy posture and attitude to copy.

***

39. Wise words from Karate 6th Dan Bill Hollister.

The principles may be unchanging but everything
else is. Keep an open mind and test ideas for yourself.

Training with weapons ensures co-ordination of both hands - through the connection of weapon, they learn to be in harmony.

Weapons training ensures that both sides of the body are trained.

Weight and length of the wooden long weapons ensures the receptive body can train and adapt to avoid inefficient posture.

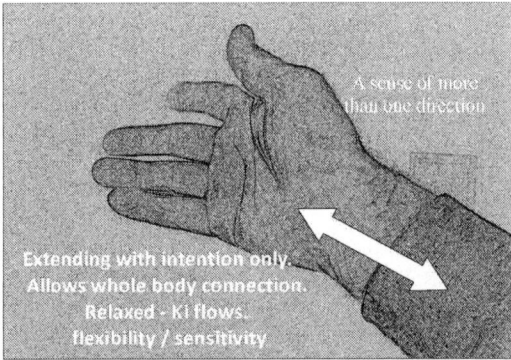

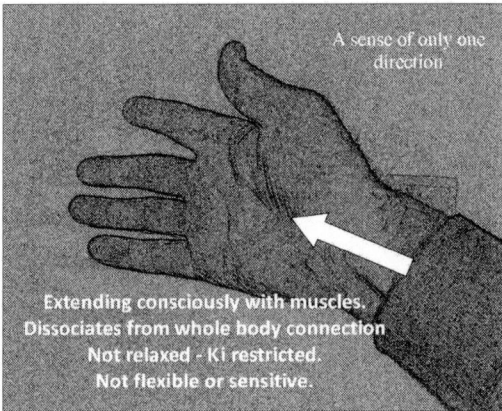

A sense of more than one direction

Extending with intention only. Allows whole body connection. Relaxed - Ki flows. flexibility / sensitivity

A sense of only one direction

Extending consciously with muscles. Dissociates from whole body connection Not relaxed - Ki restricted. Not flexible or sensitive.

40.   Extending with intention.

41.   Jo and its origins.

Miyamoto Musashi was Japan's greatest ever swordsman and put many duellists in an early grave.

Legend tells us that Muso Gonnosuke Katsuyoshi defeated him with a wooden stick (Jo). In so doing, he gave birth to a martial arts system that would elevate the humble wooden staff to one of the pre eminent weapons of the bugei (combat techniques) of Japan.

***

42.   Safety first.

Jo – almost any stick will do for practising your own moves and choreography, however, for partner work, particularly Jo dori and Jo nage, an oak Jo is less likely to break. A broken Jo can become a razor sharp dagger. Small splinters can spread on the mat. Even an oak Jo should be checked carefully for damage before each use.

Sense of energy in all directions but focus may be on only one.

Extreme Yin

Balance, Harmony, Peace Centre

Extreme Yang

43.   A picture of harmony.

A few practical Jo reminders.

Lone practice can lead to an imagined world of greatness.

Partner practice can lead to a new reality – a reality where ability, posture, spirit and timing are all put to question.

Progressively your greater skills lead to having fun, fun for the ego as Jo whacks Jo and you win. Conversely sadness when you lose …. But there'll always be a next time - or so you think.

Then a reminder comes your way that Aiki means harmony of spirit, and that your path is to beat the enemy within, not the one without.

Try not to strain the body when practising, as best you can remain relaxed and in good posture.

Good posture requires good foundations.

Hold the Jo firmly but not so tightly that it creates tensions, neither so loosely that it can be knocked from your hands.

Little finger should be able to grip comfortably.

Remember that it is not the Jo that does the work but you. The Jo is merely an extension of the body.

Blend, deflect or neutralise your partner while retaining your own power, which remains hidden from them until the moment of application.

At the point of application never feel your own power coming back to you. Only your 'opponent' or partner should experience your power.

Do not think of winning … or losing…. Merely make the correct movements that lead to the proper conclusion. It is your journey and not the destination you should keep an eye on.

Keep your thumbs and fingers safe !

Fighting distance and blending skills will all benefit from Jo practice. The power and possibilities of an opponent wielding a Jo serve to sharpen the mind.

Minimise movement – don't add your own flowery bits….. keep it simple.

In general the hips should move before the Jo.

All movement starts from the centre.

Don't over commit --- every move you make should be recoverable. This can relate to your own position or one you have in relation to your partner.

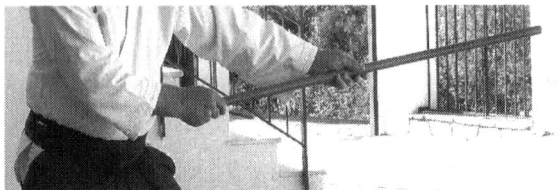

Safe practice means avoiding attacks to throat, knee, groin, jaw bone etc, martially these are the very targets you would seek .... But this conflicts with Aiki.

Place your spirit in the Jo, this connects you to its very end and not just where you are gripping it.

Give 80% effort, saving something for yourself, give less than 50% effort and you waste your time.

Hard training is not necessarily training hard ... put your whole self into the study, mind body and spirit ... look to see how you could improve, feel how you could improve ... and do it.

Using weapons correctly can develop good, habit formed, integrity of posture that is transferable to empty hand techniques. It is a key purpose behind weapons practice . . . to cultivate and develop the body and not merely to become a sword or stick fighter.

Similar advice is given below, a worth while repetition. Good advice deserves repetition.

***

45. Positioning and strength of grip on Jo.

Always add a spiral for added power, even if unnoticed by observers. Use body not arms. Remain centred, extending Ki in different directions (your body will willingly join in with your mind intent)

Remain relaxed but connected throughout your body as well as in movement. Internal power can be enhanced by cross body connection. Extend spirit beyond end of Jo. Avoid feeling your own power regardless of how great it might feel - when you can feel it, it can be used against you. You don't even have to grip the Jo to move your opponent. When feet, hips, shoulders and hands are in harmony with the alignment of the Jo and you remain centred, you maximise your soft power. (Upside down U with legs and hips idea.) Use of hips may be easier understood by thinking 'hip crease'.

Remember that the hand grip on the jo should be soft enough that someone can turn it in your hands but tight enough that they cannot take it from you.

If at any time you feel the need to prepare - then you were never ready !

***

46. How and why to train with Jo and Ken in Aikido.

It's much easier to understand thoughts than it is to write them down, but I'll have a try. We can only believe what our mind accepts and only feel what our body allows. Please explore this section and see how much you might or might not find agreeable. Everything in here can be tested by yourself, therefore you can make up your own mind of its worth.

O-Sensei must have trained with and used weapons like Jo and Ken, (also spear and bayonet) for a reason. He developed techniques to counter weapons too and more than a few of the taijutsu techniques have their origins in this field. If you do not have a partner skilled in the use of weapons then how can you hope to develop such skills as O-Sensei yourself?

As a student of aikido, isn't O-Sensei's word good enough for you or are you only looking for part of his art? (Perhaps I am guilty of this too in my pursuit of weapons training.) How can our martial art be complete without at least some weapons training?

Practising with weapons can also simply be great fun, and why should it not be so? Why not smile and be happy?

Weapons practice is something you can do almost anywhere, either alone or with a partner. (walking stick, umbrella, broom handle etc) Hiring halls and having expensive mats is not a requirement.

You have as much freedom with weapons as the art of aikido may have whispered to your soul when you first took up the art. (Garden, beach, forest – but beware Public places in case the armed response unit is called by overzealous busy-bodies . . . true story)

I hesitate to put in a 'do not', for it is rarely if ever helpful, but, if you only use your arms to move the weapons then you are merely enjoying or enduring some exercise, you will not be doing aikido. Your whole body needs to be connected and involved and better still, your mind as well. Do not isolate your arms from the rest of you.

Act from the centre, not the extremities.

Although we are told to move from the centre it is a more usefully applied mechanism to engage with the hip joint by mindfully emphasising the 'kua' or hip crease.

Training with weapons teaches your body a wide ranging variety of co-ordinated and flowing movements that can prepare you for the dynamic changes of postures required during tai jutsu.

Sensei Sergei Stoliarov

Using weapons correctly can develop good, habit formed, integrity of posture that is transferable to empty hand techniques. It is a key purpose behind weapons practice . . . to cultivate and develop the body and not merely to become a sword or stick fighter

Weapons help teach 'open' postures and offer a more narrow, smaller target to the attacker but allow greater reach and generate greater power for the defender. Training with weapons is a useful mechanism to develop correct connection through your body and also to extend your mind. Ask yourself, "When I lift Ken or Jo above my head, can I relax my shoulders any more than they are . . . even just a little?"

If the answer is 'yes' then, when you lifted the weapon, you disconnected your arms from your body in the 'energetic' connective sense. You also moved the shoulder joint from a place of its own relaxed centre to a place of extremes. Weapons or not, properly relaxed and centred joints are an asset if not essential for good aikido. Weapons can help you find this place; a place that encourages internal power to exist and energetic power to flow.

Using weapons can develop an efficient and natural gripping that maximises your potential at a level you may not have yet considered. The 5 'fingers' are controlled by two separate nerve systems. The little finger and ring finger are connected by the ulna nerve; other fingers are not connected to the ulna nerve but to a separate system. The little finger system is more active than the first finger system; activation of the little finger tends towards mind body relaxation, the feet flatten and the inner thigh muscles release. Whereas, use of the thumb, first and middle fingers causes the body to become substantial, the feet to press into the ground and inner thigh muscles to contract the body in action. Gripping with little finger first also embodies a sense of gripping from your own centre.

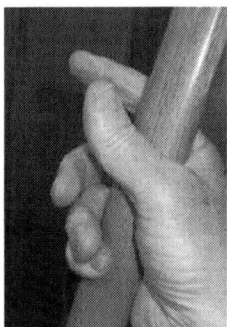

When using aiki weapons, when we lift we need a relaxed grip and relaxed body and the grip tends to be from little fingers first, roundly encompassing the Jo or Ken ...... even during the strike the hands are comfortable and relaxed as is the body, ... Then as the 'strike' materializes all changes, a fuller grip engaging thumb and first two fingers develops. Power is issued from a fully active and substantial body. However, you should always seek calm and relaxation because real power resides there.

Using ken and Jo develops circles and spirals which due to exaggeration of movement can more clearly be observed thus enhancing benefits and correcting faults.

Weapons training increases awareness and martial attitude as well as developing a greater understanding in fighting distance or *ma-ai.*

(e.g., Katate toma uchi can deliver a head strike from 3 metres or 12 feet.)

Weapons also greatly increase awareness of consequences: - is the Jo or ken safely parried or is the thumb or wrist broken? This is a fine line indeed.

Facing fears helps to develop better self control and the student's reaction speeds are necessarily improved.

Lifting the ken or Jo can also be good for your general health, especially if carried out correctly, consciously and combined with breath. Any exercise that involves raising arms and breathing in, is good for the internal organs. (Compare with some Chi Kung exercises.) The arms should remain powerful, not by muscular tension but by a power motivated by the mind; they become the 'iron bar in cotton wool'. Arms are neither collapsed nor rigid but have found a middle way that is more born of mind than physicality. It is the relaxed concentration you may have heard about before. There is extension in the feeling at all times, even when the arms are bent they do not 'come back' to you. If your arm is soft (collapsing) it will be pushed back to you and if your arm is rigid it will be used to push you back.

If you extend your arm with intention it is still possible to bend it, as long as you maintain extension and an opening in the joints (thus only appearing to observers that it comes back to you). There is a world of difference. The overall length of the arm should stay the same regardless of any change in elbow angle.

Weapons training will teach you relaxation in movement while under pressure. For example:- in the 3rd kumitachi the more relaxed the defensive strike is made, the more powerful a deflection it makes on the attacker's own strike. There is a case for, less muscle – more power. Cease to look outside for the effect of weapons but look in to yourself, and experience the effect. Seek to be one with the universe and do not fixate on any weapon for it can do nothing without the person behind it.

Finally, perhaps this can also help.

Ai Ki Do. Ki is the so called magical ingredient and becomes seemingly more so to those who feel its effects without understanding them.

Ki is the essence of the art and the essence of a powerful, healthy body. You'll have to think of it what you will; there are lots of 'definitions' and opinions out there. Just keep it simple and know that there is some force at work which you might be able to harness to your advantage. Searching for it is part of your journey.

I'll call it 'spirit energy'; Ki is real and can, from the application of mind on a relaxed body, create a physical effect merely by its presence. Importantly, it does not work the other way – any tense physical activity actually stifles or shuts down the flow of Ki. There are lots of exercises that emphasise this point. I am sure you will know many yourselves; unbendable arm is a well known example. The objective of practising such exercises is surely to develop them in a manner that can be useful to you in your martial art or in daily life.

When you pick up the ken or Jo, add nothing more to that effort than that which is required to lift or move the weapon. By adding no extra, which becomes a stifling force, your energy can flow. Remember, it is the flow of this energy which animates real power (not strength, which is very different from power). Your energy can flow from your centre all the way to your hands and beyond. By training in weapons you can access a useful tool to develop this mechanism. This is experientially true, regardless of what you really think about Ki.

My advice? Put the Ki in your aikido and put good weapons training back in while you are at it

O-Sensei surely didn't use weapons for nothing.

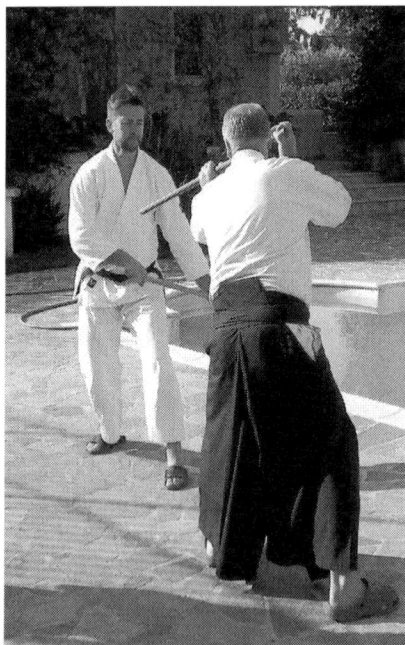

Sergei Stoliarov (left) Tony Sargeant sensei (right)

47.   On training with weapons.

The following is my interpretation of advice given me in a conversation with my friend, Karate 6th Dan Sensei William Hollister (founder of Tamar Tai Chi).

From a viewpoint of the aikido student, it would be hard to differ in opinion.   What do you think?

Understand the weapon you are using or facing. Take into account if it is bladed or blunt. Consider this, even when using wooden 'bladed' weapons. You cannot 'cut' with a blunt weapon; however, its action may follow a similar line at times in order to better protect your own wrists and joints. With weapons you learn about blocks . . . whether they are useful or instead should be deflections.

Angles of attack and defence vary with the type of weapon.

Using weapons conditions the body, developing endurance, balance, power and co-ordination. It is a conditioning that only requires the presence of self and the weapon; this is one of its advantages.

Using weapons trains the mechanics of the body; weapons are a very useful aid to developing good footwork and maintaining centre.

Imagery, using your mind, of an opponent is required in the beginning to create correct focus, posture and movement. Flailing about with the weapon without such thought will be of little benefit.

Develop control; i.e. stop where and when you want to, and not when the weapon decides.

Hit what you aim for, even if imaginary. Know what to strike, when training alone use mirror imagery.

When training, be delicate and conscious; do not miss out any of the ingredients. There should be no weakness in your actions. . . none at all.

Consider the origins.

Original intent may have come from weapon to weapon.

If training a Kata, and there are many and various, know what it's all about; know why it is this or that move.

Have purpose in your Kata . . . always know 'why'.

Weapons training will reinforce the importance and necessity of mental focus.

A relaxed mind and body will come from much training.

Extension of body is good but tension in body is not.

Weapons training can enhance the awareness of breath in the whole issue. Breath is required as part of movement.

Kiai can become part of this; however, I suspect there is still much more for us to know on this topic, in that kiai should be there to take the opponent's mind and not your own. Neither should it create a tension in your own body but instead, in theirs.

***

"In the hands of a serious student, weapons are a pathway and a prayer towards balance and peace."
    My good friend Terry, (Karate 4th Dan)

***

48.   Tai chi and Aiki principles.

Mind moves body same as Tohei's exercises.
Push using inside muscles not outer and later push using energy.
Push resistance when using 'two bodies' (there are 5 levels !)
Being heavy through being light – only feet feel weight.
Use of hip crease (kua) more to it than obvious.
Avoiding double weighting (when all feels the same)
Joints open, muscles relaxed.
Using your body affects another's body.
Respecting the attacker
Avoiding direct action on the point of contact.
Power of connected relaxation … Jo parry.

Ideas on unifying the body posture to generate more power …. more power means less effort … believe it or not.
The ideas shown below are my own, so don't blame my teachers. However, it does fit with what we call an 'internal' art.
Firstly though, the knees . . . made to move more or less in one direction or plane. The knee joint will not be comfortable if bent in other directions or twisted .. ask your own knees, they will tell you.
     So my advice is to align the knee centre with the middle of the foot . . . the long toes.

Photo on the right, below:- I'm trying to show that you can set up a 'circle of connection and therefore power between the opposite arm and hip, i.e. right hip and left arm as shown in the picture. The same is done for the other opposites (right arm and left hip). It is hard to explain but I'll try ... the hip crease is drawn in a little but the feeling has to be that it is still opening .. almost as if it feels it is going forward, which results in the energy making an arc .... part going to the ground and part raising the ribs slightly. I think this is valid but represents my opinion only.

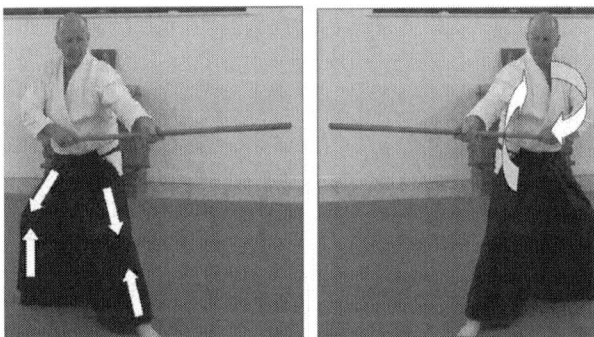

An attempt to show internal power connections in Tsuki

***

49. **Ideomotor effects** are involuntary motor movements that are performed by a person because of expectations, suggestions or preconceptions.

The person is not aware that they are causing the movements; therefore they ascribe the movement to an external force or power. The movement feels unnatural.

The "external forces" perceived are usually thought of as being paranormal in nature.

50. Historical significance - the staff

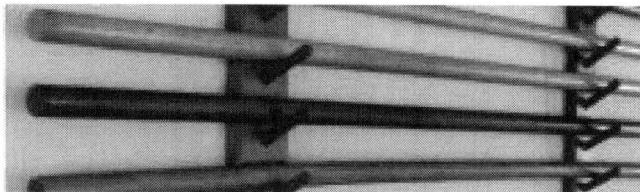

The short wooden staff - throughout history one of man's greatest friends.

To test the depth of water, reach high berries and fruits, an aid to walking and climbing, a tool, a weapon, something to raise to the heavens and connect with the Gods. Shepherds carried them, great warriors carried them, men of all persuasions.

Find that connection with nature and history .

51. Uke's grip can teach bad habits.

Shouldn't be any struggle in gripping and no joint should be pushed to the edge. No stress on body but just relaxed harmony throughout. No message sent either to self or opponent.

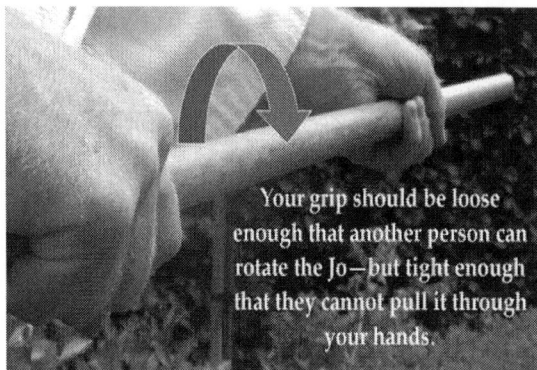

Your grip should be loose enough that another person can rotate the Jo—but tight enough that they cannot pull it through your hands.

52. Something to consider on 'being centred;'

What is it that we understand about being centred? We surely have heard our teachers say, 'be grounded, be centred'. What is 'being centred'? Well, there are some obvious observations; the body should be upright and the centre of gravity should fall comfortably in the middle of the posture. The further you lean or shift your centre of gravity to one extreme or the other the less stable you are and the harder it is to execute fast moves like turning etc.

Perhaps there is more to it than the physical; take the eyes for example, not possible to move them into the back of your head physically ... but you can with the mind. Your eyes should be soft, soft focussed and appear to your mind that they are further back in your head ... near the ears .. and are looking out through the eye sockets from within and not from the front edge.

A mental sense of energy going in all directions also assists centring, front, back, left, right, up and down ... your intention may be focussed in a particular direction ... as in Tsuki (thrust) but the sense that your energy expands from the centre in all directions should also exist.

Centred is also about being calm ... an essential feature of our art .... if not calm then you will be reaching out to one extreme or another ... it will fail to be balanced .. centred. When you move your centre towards an opponent, they will sense the intent.

***

53. The student and the tatami – just one point of view among many.

'Hey, you haven't got any mats down.'

No, tonight we are practising weapons techniques, if it involves a throw we control to point of balance. It's quite simple. When their balance is taken they are no longer a threat.

'I can't train without mats.'

Why not? Why must you have mats?

'So we don't get hurt when we are thrown.'

Why do you have to be thrown? Aren't some of the techniques locks, even kotegaeshi can be used as a gently but persistently applied lock, it doesn't have to involve a throw and a high fall.

'You've only got to watch aikido on Youtube and you can see you need mats. . . otherwise the uke would be hurt due to the power of the throw.'

So, why does aikido require such hard throws? Isn't it good enough to harmonise, take uke's balance and gently place them in a position where they realise attack is futile?

'It's good fun to be thrown on the mat, gets the adrenalin going; makes you feel good.'

And how old are you now, do you think you will think the same when you are in your fifties, sixties, seventies? Or is aikido only for young, fit and able people?

'We don't have any old people in our dojo so that doesn't apply, it's not for wimps; it's a martial art.'

Aha, a martial art? So what was the prime ethos of the founder then?

'Who?'

The founder of aikido, the one we call O-Sensei and

bow to at the beginning of every class.

'Ah, yes, move out of the way, take control and apply technique until they tap to surrender.'

So it wasn't this then?

"Aikido is not a technique to fight with or defeat the enemy. It is the way to reconcile the world and make human beings one family. "

Morihei Ueshiba, Founder of Aikido.

Can't you do that without mats?

Written by some old chap who has taught weapons for over 5 years in a hall without mats.

***

Speed and power come from relaxation and co-ordination— not from strength

***

54.   Value of weapons by Tony Sargeant 6th dan Aikikai

"For over 45 years I have trained with weapons as fifty percent of my practice. O-Sensei clearly trained with weapons, yet over my years of aikido training I have had to listen to the diverse arguments over the need or not to train with them.

Now, I have reached a point in my training, where I no longer need them to aid my own practise – they have already done their job.

I realise that concentrating on body movements does not develop the footwork as well as training with weapons. Nage often struggles to find correct footwork in taijutsu but had they taken up weapons training, their footwork would have become automatic and allowed a deeper understanding of the art to be reached.

I do not think O-Sensei used weapons just because he liked them.'

Over the years many students have requested a Jo class, because they find the freedom of expression and variance of use with the Jo much more interesting than the ken.

I realise from this that we have let our students down by not clearly stating the purpose behind weapons training. We owe it to our teachers, masters like Saito Sensei to honour the founder's teaching, just as he did. Saito Sensei asked us to keep the art alive and safe – and this meant the weapons legacy too.

If you really have an interest in following O-Sensei but your own style does not train in weapons, there are clips on youtube to watch and after that it is up to you to find time and space. It will be worth it.

Apart from the essential footwork emphasised and instilled by weapons, there are other gifts too.

Receiving an all out attack from a weapon allows you to come to terms with panic and fear and guide you to correct positioning with an adversary. Without pressurised training such as this you will never know if your version of the art will work in the street. It may be too late by then.

The photo shows a completed move but the power, stability of hips and feet, allow mind and body to become one with the attacker. It is not *seen* but it is *felt* by both – to me this is O-Sensei's gift and why weapons should be part of your training."

***

55. Same as the Dodo - is Aikido's goose cooked?

I've been practising aikido since about 1974 and I'm only just beginning to develop a new and worthwhile understanding. I've seen people who I believe really understand the essence of aikido, though I still struggle to find the way they achieve it. I would like to share what I now know with anyone who is interested. Therein lies the problem – no one is! I teach Aiki weapons, Jo and Ken and have done as a

dedicated weapons class since 2008. These isolated years of training and exploring have opened up new and rewarding insights.

It's about connection within self, about victory over self, overcoming the habits and reactions that we unerringly developed over the years to our detriment. The greatest power comes from relaxation. The lightest touch of thumb and forefinger on the Jo can overcome almost any opposing physical strength. To understand this, it is required to understand what is meant by relaxation. Videos and books can rarely if ever express the essence of the art of aikido, though they may on occasions show you a suitable gateway. Once again, a recurring theme shows itself, what you really need is not what it appears to be. In fact what you desire, you can have, by doing the opposite of what you think you need. Never add strength, if anything, remove strength to find real power. Opposites have immense power, as does relaxation. However, the key to much success will come from your **mind** –

your greatest friend and
yet your greatest enemy.

You must learn alone but, to do so, you need the company of others.

Our modern, progressive world with all its impatient information and frenzied, tense activity finds little time for an inner journey that takes a lifetime . . . or more.

Eventually, this could draw people into a dark

age of wide spread mental illnesses . . . and there may not be a lamp left burning for them to find their way out.

Aikido has a beneficial spiritual quality, or at least it should have.

Even if O-Sensei's aikido dies out and its bones lie in the ashes with those of the Dodo, my own personal journey does not feel as though it was wasted, despite the disappointment of no new students to enjoy the same.

***

56.   Can we disappear?

I've put some thought into this. . . but am minded of an old saying,

> *"all ye who search for certainty,*
> *abandon hope."*

In Wudang mountain a Taoist monk once said to the visiting students, "seeing is not seeing." In that fortunately receptive moment I understood what he meant. **Illusion;** almost all is illusion, all colour that we see is not real, it is an illusion created by our mind so that we can distinguish our environment.

Our sight is illusion too in that the 'blind spot' that we all have in our eyes cannot be found by trying to find it in the space in front of us. The brain knows that something should be there and creates an image that fills the blind spot. The blind spot has disappeared from our vision. When you look in the mirror you rarely see yourself as you really are, you see an image that is your perception of who you think you are.

Magicians work their magic and make things disappear in front of our eyes; it is a trick, our mind sees what it thinks the eyes have seen and if the eyes have missed something, then the brain just makes something up that fits.

I read somewhere that when attacked, **O-Sensei seemed to disappear**, much to the surprise of the attacker. Note that to the observer, nothing of the sort seemed to happen, therefore we can presume that it has something to do with the impression felt by the attacker alone.

My own novice view is that this surprise was multi layered.

Let's consider the implications for our own learning if we want to emulate O-Sensei's skills. What he did, we may never know. What he might have done, we can explore.

Perhaps Uke is distracted; by a movement across his eye-line. A 'temporary blinding' either because their sight is obstructed or that their eyes followed the movement and took their mind with it; if their mind has gone from where nage was and followed something else ... then has nage 'disappeared'?

Eyes are an essential component of your power, your ability and your understanding. We can test this easily by pushing on someone who stands in good posture and whose eyes are looking forward, yet when they look down they are more easily moved. . . their eyes and their intention are no longer one with their body.

The next thing to consider is the simple physical level. This is where you don't visually disappear but physically to the Uke you feel like you have.

Uke directs a force towards Nage and makes contact, this satisfies Uke that his purpose is being fulfilled. . . as long as certain criteria are met by Nage that is. Retaining the point of contact Nage can withdraw his body and neutralise the force.

Neutralise is the better description than deflect or avoid

or any other word that you might substitute. Uke's body experience is that everything is alright and going to plan, Uke has put the force exactly where they wanted and it has not been interfered with, therefore they continue with what to the observer is a senseless strike. . . however, Uke's eyes tell a different tale, all has gone wrong, they have missed their target. Their target is no longer where they thought it was, it has 'disappeared'. The strange thing is we trust our body more than our eyes and the Uke inexplicably continues to apply force in their chosen direction; Uke cannot feel any hard resistance but is aware that there is still 'something' inexplicably tangible there to push; so they do, to no avail. For Nage's part they have retained a passive presence at the point of contact while being active in moving the rest of their body, storing their own power as they do so. Nage is active in setting up their own posture and energy to advantage at the same time as Uke's attack is failing.

Where Nage places their Ki or imagination is important and you should not be surprised if it is in a direction totally against logical thought. . . for logical thought has no place in this 'magic'. Keep an open mind on this and explore it for yourself. The Chinese have that lovely saying, "don't listen to what they say, go see."

Perhaps O-Sensei had surpassed these methods and was using an 'energy' level technique. We shouldn't really call it technique either as it is closer to 'magic; something few understand but at which many marvel.

The placing of one's mind outside the body can create a tangible, if subtle, presence which influences something in another person. Isn't this the 'Ki' in Aikido?

O-Sensei said that he was aware that these things happened but could not explain it. It is not really something anyone can explain or intellectualise, simply something that you 'know' exists when you 'experience' it.

My own valued and respected teacher, Sensei Tony Sargeant is not only a dedicated student of O' Sensei's aikido but has studied Tai Chi, Yoga, Healing Arts and Meditation. All of these can open portals of understanding through personal experience. During training sessions, when Sensei Tony offered his arm up to uke (initiating) it was almost impossible not to reach out to grab or push it. As soon as you did, his arm seemed to disappear, leaving a hole in space into which you were drawn. As many of you will know, this is no easy task to accomplish; try it. It was many years ago when I experienced this and to this day I cannot achieve it myself.

I am beginning to think that Ki is real, it has a tangible existence, it can be felt, experienced, sensed, it can be used to influence others. This is such a difficult subject to write about mainly because of my limited ability and knowledge. . . but it's not going to stop me trying and perhaps you will know it better.

You need to be able to shift your consciousness around and out of your body. Koichi Tohei's exercise using the Jo is an excellent example. With a partner in Tsuki No Kamae (basic tsuki stance) hold the end of the Jo with only a light grip and put your spirit into the far end of the Jo, the end that your partner is holding. The difference between spirit close to you and spirit extended away from you is great. You can test this for yourself.

Practice putting your consciousness elsewhere in the body, e.g. the ball of the foot, or the palm of the hand. Control over transferring consciousness is used in pain relief. You twist a toe on the mat. . . you can keep your mind on the toe and all its pain or shift your consciousness to e.g. palm of the hand or to your hara or centre. Not easy, so you need practice.

Meditation can assist you in such control. The pain disappears ! It is as if it were not there. Herein lays the clue to what we need to do in order to disappear.

I just hope you can find a way through these ramblings to an understanding which will be of value to you.

Try and think this way. . . there is no such thing as imagination. . . everything is real.

Whatever you 'imagine' exists, does exist.

To feel the subtlety of Ki try this exercise. Ask a partner to place their hand on your arm near the shoulder. They should push only lightly but steady.

Stand relaxed but with life. Put your consciousness in your head behind the third eye, sense that this place opens and becomes alive. Move to the heart area and do the same thing with your consciousness, keep both centres open and alive. Now move to the Hara or centre, bring that consciousness here too, open and alive, keeping all three points open and alive. . . . it is all you think about . . no wondering, no doubt just stick to what you have been asked to do. Your partner who is applying the gentle push should feel like you at first 'disappeared' or at least became softer, and then they should feel like their whole body is gently and subtly being moved away from you.

When you are one with the universe,
the universe will help you.

In the ken partner practice of Ki Musubi No Tachi, as the attacker lifts to strike for the second time there is a point during which they are unsighted from your ken. You then enter in migi hamni with Tsuki to their chest. If you have the timing correct it is they who expose your ken to their awareness as they lift their own ken. It suddenly appears, giving them a surprise which you can see reflected in their startled body language; my point is that there are things that appear and disappear and it is this phenomena we could use to advantage. . . if we have the skill. The mind is nearly everything in this matter; that and the perfect timing born of good training.

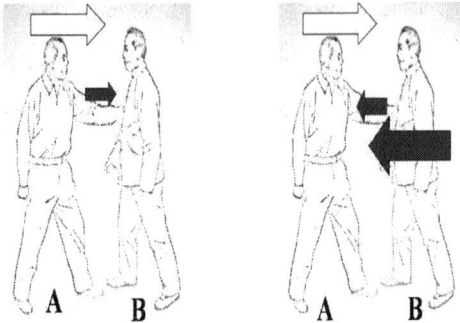

If 'A' walks towards 'B' with energy and intention to push and then withdraws the physical push at the last moment, before contact, 'B' usually senses the energy and leans in to counter it. Of course it isn't there, only the belief exists that it is. Is that not disappearing too?

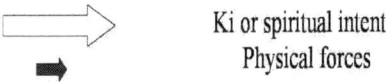

Ki or spiritual intent
Physical forces

Without exploration much remains undiscovered

A's intent, energy and movement

B's intent energy

In this first case we have yang against yang, strength against strength and the strongest wins.
However, the following ideas do not rely upon strength.

Second case, A's intent is to push B to the star point. If B then puts his consciousness and intent to the same place. A should feel B soften and what A thought he was pushing disappears

Third case. A pushes as before but B places his consciousness in his centre. (Hara, DanTien, centre. Again A senses that what he thought he was pushing has changed, it no longer seems to be there in the form it was at the start. 'Something' has disappeared

A pushes B and B 'accepts' the energy, absorbing it until it is all neutralised. B may not have disappeared but may seem to be immovable.
A has little left to push with and senses this loss.

All of these ideas, which you can try for yourself, involve the mind. . . Your mind. By shifting your consciousness to a place outside your body 'something' of you will have disappeared as far as the consciousness of the person pushing goes.

***

105

57. What is your opinion on cross training within and without the art of Aikido ?

Of course we cannot ask everyone, as half the aikido teachers have made a choice already and won't be reading this, and in all likelihood nor will many of the students of those that do. That does have a convenience to it for some, I am sure.

Did you train with other styles of aikido, or even with different teachers of the same style?

Did you train in other arts which taught you something of benefit to your own study of aikido? This could be a positive benefit in understanding or negative in that you realised this other art added nothing to your own learning. (Most unlikely.)

If you never tried other styles or arts are you sure that your aikido is the best it can be?

Are you confident that what you do cannot be bettered from a source other than your own teacher and style?

Have you ever wondered why some schools will never respond to you, let alone train with you? (Perhaps they are very happy and successful in their own cult like bubble, so why should anyone else mind.)

Are you convinced only your way is true to O-Sensei? Did he actually ask you to copy him or did he ask you to embrace the principles and develop the art?

Develop it. . . not ruin it!

Do you encourage your students to attend courses and workshops by other teachers?

If not, why not? (It is usually a given that lower

grades benefit from a grounding in one style before looking at another so as not to confuse. There are plenty of high grades out there who are confused too.)

If you are a student, why don't you attend workshops and seminars by other teachers?

Are you afraid you won't learn anything?

Are you afraid you will?

Wasn't aikido about reconciling the world in peace? You won't find that by building walls, will you?

I do believe that the great masters of the art of aikido had more than a brief dabble in other arts, arts which taught them something very few will find in aikido alone. Unless you think aikido is something that I don't. My own teacher and his before him always encouraged us to go and see others and to take away that which was helpful, discarding that which was not. Such teachers are not afraid.

Are you annoyed by these questions because your stuff works okay?

***

58   Exploring the point of contact.

I'm sure that many of you will already know a great deal more about the point of contact principles. Let us travel together a while and see where we might agree and help each other.

Surely principles in aikido unite us, even if some princip<u>als</u> may not. It's a paradox that followers of aikido sometimes fail to engage in its philosophy with other clubs, teachers or styles. This is a route to conflict and disharmony – how strange is that?

I've picked a Jo nage technique just to illustrate my current understanding about the point of contact. We all know that written articles cannot transmit perfect understanding; there's no surprise that this one's no different.

The photo shows the technique half way through and about the place where movement can often become difficult for nage, a place where they may be tempted to add force to the point of contact and so become the attacker.

If nage feels the struggle at this point then they

must be in conflict and therefore not Aiki.

They are in conflict with their partner, in conflict in their own mind and in conflict within their own body. Ego, the need to be the winner, the greater enemy living within, can prevent effective aiki. Human beings usually enjoy the feel of their own power, that desire can cause problems. (It begins the moment a baby first presses their feet against the floor – they just love that feeling). At any time you feel your own power realise that you only feel it because it is coming back to you. If it's coming back to you it is available for your opponent to use against you. At the point where you no longer feel your own physical power returning, (note carefully that this does not mean collapsing, retreating or giving in – in fact the opposite will become true) the energy of the attacker is absorbed, dissipated and confused for they no longer know where to apply their own force.

We can retain the point of contact for sensitivity but we should not act directly upon it. Breathing and maintaining centre is protective in itself, no extra power should be added to the point of contact as that can be self defeating. If you conflict at the point of contact the opponent will know your intention and power, in reality they are just as capable of using that information as you are.

In general, mindfully acting on the point of contact only results in conflict and struggle, often this means that the strongest will win. Also if you disturb the attacker in their chosen action then they will change how and what they do. e.g. a blocked hand might invite an elbow strike instead. (This 'non compliance' would rarely be countenanced in an aikido class, which is a shame as it relates to an important principle).

Let them go where they think they want to go, let them think they are successful – in fact let them **feel** that they have succeeded. Though their eyes will clearly tell them that they have failed, their body tells them otherwise. The mind will almost inevitably believe body over sight and the attacker will ignore the truth told by their eyes.

Back to our specific Jo nage example; a sincere, uncompromising and mindful use of, in this case, the right hip results in a harmony at the point of contact with the attacker. It also allows retention of a balanced centre throughout. Everything moves around that centre and remains the case whether using the hips or stepping.

There should be no slack in the body, or mind either, as you should be as one, united in principles; a relaxed concentration with open joints should permeate your entire body, in relaxation, energy can flow. Major blocking points for our own energy are shoulders, neck and hips; the block is caused by tension. For all the skills of many Aikidoka, their own understanding of body awareness is often sparse or non existent. I believe this to be an error in many of our studies and may well find correction in Ki style exercises and some mind/body meditations too.

Avoid putting your own mind at the point of contact; and deprive them of any messages of conscious intent. If the opponent is unaware of the intention or location of your power then they will find it difficult to respond. Remember, they will believe their body over their eyes. To enable whole body power at the physical level and this is where body awareness comes in, you need to cross connect your body, i.e. opposite arms and hips. This cross connection of the body creates great internal power – why would you not want it? There is nothing wrong with being powerful, just take care how you use it.

How often has the teacher said, "use your hips"?

How often has the teacher said,
"this is how to use your hips."?

How, is very important and training with weapons is a useful mechanism to exploit the understanding we need.

It's too much to go into here but the hip should feel like it is melting away, disappearing, it is not a solid feeling of engagement. It's all about body awareness and the intelligent use of mind.

Power can be delivered to the point of contact or more accurately power travels through the point of contact without force, without conflict. Providing you do not act mindfully at that point itself.

***

"The simplest technique contains
the most profound principles."

***

59.   Peace or Conflict? A choice?

O-Sensei wanted aikido to reconcile the world in peace. A noble and worthy sentiment, but is it possible? Without conflict where does your aikido get you?

"Why did he do this?"

How did he do that?

For anything to exist there must be an opposite. What you read now is dark and you are only aware of it because the background is light, if the background was dark the words would disappear . . . you need opposites for existence. You may find opposites written here, you may disagree with what is written, this too is valid.

To make progress, doing technique, forms or methods is not enough, there is something else, in fact, it is that which would appear to be the exact opposite of what you think you are studying.

"You cannot make butter by churning sand."

Let's explore just one idea for personal development in Aiki, that of opposition. The Chinese use the expressions Yin and Yang, (Yin is passive, Yang is active. From 'aikido and the Harmony of Nature' by Mitsugi Saotome. "*In Kannagara the counterparts of Yin and Yang are* aramitma, *spirit of firmness and strength, and* nigimitama, *spirit of flexibility and gentleness.*"

They are opposites but not necessarily in conflict, they complement each other in harmony. Is this not Aiki? That for which you seek?

Is it possible that at the centre between the opposing forces there is a 'magical' place where you can engage with the inner, innate you, and be in tune with the universal Ki.

We'll try and look at some practical matters but I hope you will be able to look further at how your very soul, your way of living might change too.

I'm going to presume that you have some aikido basics, in particular with the Jo. Let's use the basic thrust or Tsuki for our purpose.

Pick up your Jo or even pretend you have one, make a thrust and stay there for a while as you consider how it 'feels', your posture, your balance, your power.

In the process of making Tsuki there are many subtle movements, too many to consider here, except for the basic large physical movement forward. Remember that we said earlier that we must have an opposite? We obviously cannot match the physical forward thrust with a physical backwards one, for both of these are Yang or active. What we can use though is Yin, physically moving, no, but energetically moving, yes. Your mind, Ki, Chi, Yi, imagination, pretence, call it what you will, can project back on the same plane as the forward thrust. Your energy flows in both directions but the emphasis is backwards. . . almost like it is the propulsive force that drives the Jo physically forward.

Try your basic thrust again then project your mind back along the line that the Jo took. Stay a while and 'feel' what has happened. You should find that you are more stable, centred, and relaxed, you will be more powerful and in more than one direction. . . get someone to test you. The place you have found is that 'magic' place where the inner you resides and is at peace.

Relaxation leads to opening of the body and opening the body leads to space, the space in which the real power seems to live, the essence itself.

Ai ki do . . harmony spirit way . . . note it doesn't mention body.

Opening up the body with the mind to find the 'space' has some odd side effects, for example, it may expose old injuries that you have been shielding with tight muscle and, odd as it may seem, it can release emotional memories that were locked in the body too. (Leading to strange dreams, flashbacks and the like.)

These are the 'layers' we added to our innate self as we went through life. Practising other arts like yoga or tai chi can help to open the body and by continuing to practice through these layers you can come out the other side and be closer to who you always really were.

The journey is the goal and is ever onward; the innate in you was always there – can you find it again? To quote an old Chinese saying,

"Peace lies not in the world,
but in the man who walks the path."

So, the question was, 'peace or conflict', I think if you can access the space *between* then you can touch both and there find a harmony you otherwise would never realise existed. . . enlightenment.

***

"Ego is a false God
that too many people love to worship,
often without knowing it."

***

60. On the benefits of workshops and courses.

"This day is called the feast of Crispian: He that outlives this day, and comes safe home, will stand a tip-toe when the day is named, And rouse him at the name of Crispian. He that shall live this day, and see old age, Will yearly on the vigil feast his neighbours, And say 'To-morrow is Saint Crispian:' Then will he strip his sleeve and show his scars. And say 'These wounds I had on Crispin's day.' "
History of Henry V

Okay, so it's a bit over the top but the sentiments remain true. What can we *gain* from a workshop or seminar that goes beyond our normal class? What can we *give* too? There are many gifts; the greatest is to yourself, then there is the support you give to the local teacher and the guest teacher, a support without which clubs would eventually fall into oblivion. . . so your gift includes the perpetuation of the art. There is the gift of your own knowledge, given without ego; the gift of friendship between strangers; the gift of joy in sharing O-Sensei's art; the gift of question to the teacher who will learn from your question alone, whatever your level.

So what do we get out of it?

Mainly we get as much as we are prepared to give, it is mutual.

Without a training partner your quest is fruitless; as is a teacher without a student.

What keeps us from attending workshops? Perhaps you have sound reasons why attendance is not possible and after all it is your life in which you must do your best for all. Perhaps you have darker reasons for not attending and they relate to your own problems and insecurities. Perhaps you should question the depth to which you follow O-Sensei's ethics. I do. If you are annoyed by this then you probably don't!

I attended the 25th May Bukiwaza workshop hosted by Wellsprings Aikido in Dorset, taught by Sensei Paul McGlone of TIA Europe; the subject was 13 Jo Kata and associated awase. I was also honoured to be asked to teach at the Wellsprings Club Friday night class the night before the workshop. Teaching is one of the greatest tools to learning. . . you soon find out if you are in error. There were things I could show and those I could not, some of which I'd thought were fairly problem free. We specifically looked at the strengths and weaknesses of pins. . . but how wrong can you be when a 4th kyu so easily evades your pin. When I was younger and stronger I would have used just that to try and win but now I know I must find a path that is successful by other means.

We need errors and failures; it is what shows us the truth of the matter and it is at the heart of our learning. If we don't embrace challenge and step out of our comfort zone how can we ever progress except perhaps in our imagination.

Later that evening I had a conversation with Sensei Mark about the subject of reality in aikido and what constituted reality. It moved on to practical evasion from kihon; He gripped my wrist and I thought, 'I know too much, I will move easily and he will be surprised'; the surprise was all mine as I couldn't move. He explained that he was 'cheating' as he called it by making small changes to posture that countered my moving. Is that cheating? Is it not also a reality?

I already have much to think about and we haven't even started the Bukiwaza workshop yet.

The day of the 13 Jo kata workshop. When we arrived at the venue, a really beautiful village sports facility bathed in sunshine, some students were already there and everyone happily helped to carry in what was needed; another gift, the joy of willing people sharing a task. Some students came late, an hour late. All the way from Reading the Bank holiday traffic had taken its toll on their travels; another gift arrives, understanding, empathy, sympathy, welcoming smiles.

When asked by Sensei Mcglone, all present accepted that they already knew the 13 count Jo Kata, and we did too. . . our version of it anyway. We were asked to demonstrate as Sensei counted the moves. We received our first big correction after the very first move. Any guesses? You'll have done it at some time and almost certainly will again! Don't look down. . . your feet have been with you a long time, you shouldn't need to look when you place the tip of the Jo on the ground. Of course, silly us, we knew that didn't we? How annoying that we let ourselves down before we even started. We often 'know' something that we would correct in others and yet we fall into the same trap. . . this in itself is a giant learning point. Other corrections followed, accompanied by sound reasoning why it should be so. There are other ways but the logic of the method shown was indisputable, so lots of room for thought again. There was much emphasis on blending. . . . ah yes we know that too . . . but this was deeper than we had thought to go. It was about connecting, sensing breath, energy and intention in your partner so that you effect a true harmony and not just blend to escape. If anything it was blend to become one. Most notably in the 2nd move of the kata awase, using their energy to drive the movement of high speed turn and strike. No wasted foot movements that rob you of time, everything efficiently executed. 3rd tsuki from your partner is not blocked and almost not parried either, just softly blended and deflected. I'd been working for several months on a powerful counter deflection prior to completing the tsuki but Sensei McGlone's version didn't do this, it merely changed direction and was easily lined up for the finishing tsuki. There were many such enlightenments, all of which were ably demonstrated with accompanying explanation; though it was not needed as the effectiveness of the demonstration was evident. Key points? True blending at a deeper level, awareness, no wasted movements, know when and how to move off line as necessary, blend with the partner's energy. . . engage with it and use it to power your own sense of movement.

For me it was a wonderful weekend with the blessings of fine weather, good food, great friends and good teaching. . . it enabled me the privilege of several more steps on the spiritual pathway.

What can you get from attending a workshop?

Everything, absolutely everything, just keep an open mind about you.
You simply cannot beat, being there!

"Physical technique has a limit."

***

Section 3 Amusement Only

61. Insights for new students in Aikido.

If you are coming on our mat,
make sure that you are, not too fat,
and if you really want to win,
make sure that you are, not too thin.

If you want to learn to save,
when joining us, you need be brave.
But also useful, so I hear,
is, never lose, your sense of fear.

Always heed, the teacher wise,
then question what he does advise.
Practise well and peace you'll gain,
as long as you don't mind the pain.

Keen students fine, come through the door,
they love it all, they love the floor.
Once gi is bought with stroke of pen,
we won't be seeing them again.

On my advice, don't come to blows,
Aikido's secrets – no one knows.
Strength of gnat or strength of ox,
all Aikido - paradox.

***

62.   The new uchideshi.

Extracts of an imagined conversation at an aikido seminar, begins with self centred student . . .

"So, a little bird tells me you have an uchideshi now. . . things must be looking up at your club these days."

"Yes, we're very lucky; she has all the attributes of a master, even at her young years."

"Oh, so it's a she. What's she look like then?"

"Short, well built, fair hair, brown eyes, quite attractive actually and has a friendly tactile personality, I like her a lot."

"So, what's the missus think about that then, bit jealous eh?"

"No, my wife is very understanding and in fact gets on very well with Elsa. OK they might have fell out a couple of times but all in all we are quite happy the three of us. In fact you could learn a lot yourself from Elsa. . .

change your lifestyle it would. . . and your aikido would improve too."

"Oh yeah, of course it would. So just what's so good about this smarty pants Elsa uchideshi then that she could improve my lifestyle."

"Ok. if you really want to know; she eats a proper balanced diet that suits her body type. . . and sticks to it too ... no cheating ever. Keeps clean, likes swimming, and washes frequently. She rests at the right times. . . she realises when the body needs to regenerate and sleeps. . . no forcing herself to stay up and watch TV or check the computer for messages. In training she is energy sensitive, loyal, trustworthy, totally attentive, moves well, using the whole body in a relaxed but powerful and totally coordinated way and uses the eyes in a focussed manner. . . much like the eyes of a predator, taking everything in, missing nothing. Despite being self driven and determined she listens and follows instructions willingly, not once has she questioned my teaching, not once has she criticised me behind my back. She is an excellent student. I think she is in it for life and not for the occasional socialising like so many students can be these days. We haven't had to spend a lot of money on bedding etc as she seems happy to sleep on the floor. . . it must be good for her back or something. We have of course supplied blankets and crockery and she has the run of half the house. I strongly suspect she is highly intelligent but has never spoken to us yet about her ideas. . . . She is just totally natural with a good personality and gets on with everyone she meets".

"Sounds a right creep if you ask me. . . anyway I'm off for a beer and a pizza now . . . I'll let you know sometime if I am coming to one of your workshops.

I'd like to meet this Elsa, perhaps she'd like to come out for a drink with me. Gotta go, see ya ………"

Another student arrived, "Hi sensei, was that one of your old training partners you were just chatting with?"

"Yes, I was telling him about Elsa, our new live in student."

"I thought Elsa was your Labrador dog; did he realise you were talking about a dog?"

"You are right and no he didn't. . . but I think secretly he was so impressed by the description I gave him that he's now looking forward to taking her out! Strange thing is, she won't judge him and will probably go".

Their minds wandered briefly to the day dream world; they smiled and they laughed.

Happy days, Elsa uchideshi days.

63. Dojo, is it a place, or an instruction . . . ?

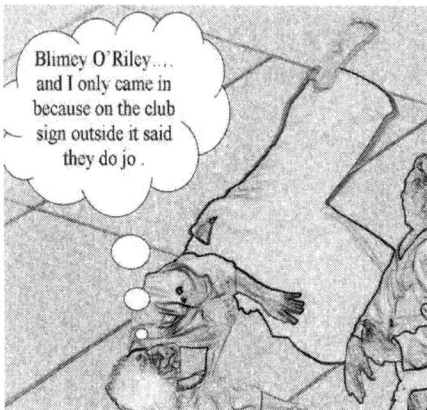

64. A tale of two Gi's

I hope you might find this a humorous tale about Gi's …. Unless of course you have one the same! (Gi; a term I am using to describe the heavy duty white pyjama like clothing as used in Judo, Karate and Aikido).

So often they seem ill fitting, and on occasions you might just wonder what sort of animal they were made for ….. Certainly not human at times I suspect.. perhaps made to fit O-Uke, the Yeti like brute you always fear will one day attend the seminar for which you have just booked, despite still sporting a slowly recovering injury.
It reminds me of many years ago when I had a peasant like job for the Government's civil engineering laboratories. Apart from a pair of rubber boots, a pencil, ruler, chair, desk and name on the shared office door, they issued me with a pair of overalls; a sort of boiler suit affair. They looked good until I tried them on and found they did not fit …. anywhere! Walking in them was difficult as the crotch of the garment was closer to my knees than my groin. 'No problem', I thought, 'just take them back to stores.'
I found the store-man and explained, "I'm sorry but these overalls don't fit me."
The simple apology and exchange I expected did not come to pass, the store-man simply looked up over his glasses and said, "I'm sorry too, but if a Ministry boiler suit fits you then you're deformed."

I've often wondered if the same applies to the Gi. (Apologies to any finely built folk out there that actually have perfectly fitting Gi.)

Somewhere in the world in a Gi factory, far, far away, the quality control manager ... on a bag of nuts a day and only part time ... is looking at a collection of misshapen but otherwise well made garments. "Mmm," he thinks, "somehow we need to get rid of this lot." He calls over an old chap, probably a foreign cousin of the Ministry store-man. "Sort these into pairs, that is a top and a bottom together and put them in plastic bags .... There's a selection of labels over there, just find one that seems about right and stick it on. I'll go and arrange shipping to the UK; they're usually a good bet for this stuff."

A few months later in the UK, an Aikidoka takes possession of his new Gi, confident in its quality as it was recommended by his teacher who said he made no profit from the sale and that he knew lots of people who wore theirs with pride and satisfaction ... mainly at other clubs apparently.

"Right, here we go," said the Aikidoka to himself standing in his Woolworth's underpants, "let's try the trousers first."

He tried to pull them up to his waist, but something was stopping them being pulled right up, ... yes ... it was his groin!

Staring down in disbelief he could see that between crotch and waist band there was only a hand's width of material. "Mmm," he pondered, as he strained to pull the cord through the waist band that was too narrow for the amount of cord, finally he manages to make a bow knot that has a remote but hopeful chance of keeping these 'hipster' style Gi trousers from slipping down, "Not to worry, the Gi top will bridge the gap."

Looking down at the crisp starch white Gi trousers he observes the knee pad patches and decides to try them out. Our Aikidoka kneels in seiza, the back of the trousers slip lower still and expose what is commonly termed 'builder's bum', and there in full view, resting nowhere near under his knees but on his upper legs are a pair of crisp starch white reinforced knee pads.

He stands and looking in the mirror consoles himself, "Oh, well, not to worry, at least the leg length is good if I fold them up a turn or two."

He consoles self yet again, "They're not too bad for thirty quid, and they do have some lovely embroidered oriental writing on the label." ..... Little does he realise that these are merely essential laundry instructions that he can never knowingly follow and not the warrior like spiritual aphorisms of aspiration as he thinks they are. Then there was the classic half hippo half kangaroo animal he saw as a beautifully embroidered dragon.

Picking up the plastic bag he tips out the Gi top. He

looks briefly at the bag before placing it on the nearby bench. It read, 'dagner extinguish life, not wearbag,'

"Crumbs," he thought, "they could do with an interpreter never mind a tailor".

The Gi jacket slipped on easily, the arms were a good length ... conveniently about the same length as his own ... the body of the jacket is comfortingly long and overlaps his low slung waist band easily. He suddenly feels good and acts out an imaginary technique in front of the all admiring mirror. He contemplates how swish he will look on the tatami in his new Gi ... 'ah, the envy of all who watch' .... he thought.

"Enough of this, young man", he says to himself, "Let's try the belt on..... See if we remember how to tie it eh?" He crossed the jacket left over right - "er, or was that right over left," he thought.

He busied himself watching his hands wrap the belt around his body twice and then make several attempts to have a flat knot that pointed in the right direction. At last it was done, mind you there seemed to be almost enough spare belt left over for another trip around his midriff. Still, perhaps he would grow into it, you know, develop a good centre as they say.

Dressing now complete he eagerly anticipated admiring his latest martial attire in the mirror, oh, how good he felt, how magnificent he would be at class, he could hardly wait.

Then horror of all horrors, the image that looked back at him from the mirror was not remotely how he had seen it in his mind. The Jacket was fine at the bottom but at the top it didn't meet at all, leaving half an acre of hairy chest exposed. Even tugging it from both sides did not help ... it was just simply short of material.

Even at his level he could envisage a new and unexpected life experience on the mat, as while his scrunched waist band cut mercilessly into his hips and with his Sensei's voice ringing in his ears, "get those trousers shortened before you lose a toe in them," some gorilla like uke would be tearing out handfuls of chest hair instead of gripping his gaping lapels.

 Oh well, not to worry, at least it was a lot better than his previous Gi.

65. Not just Gi's apparently !

I read the Gi tale, had a really good laugh, you have to have trained in martial arts to really appreciate how true it is. It reminded me when I once bought a 'box' through my club sensei, 'these are the ones to wear' he told me, 'great protection'. I was not sure, everybody had cloth pouches and this one was mesh, he assured me it was the one for me.(even though he did not wear this sort himself). Oh well I thought, it must be ok. I wore it twice before all the mesh started to tear and fall to pieces. This is not right, I thought, as everyone else was saying they bought theirs from a magazine for half the price, and they were cloth, in fact everyone's was cloth. So I took it back to my sensei and showed him the problem! 'What have you been doing with this?' he said. 'Just wearing it', I answered. 'You must sweat a lot', he said. (I thought everyone did). Perhaps you can sew it together,' then I complained about it being uncomfortable. He looked confused, so I said, 'don't worry.'

'No,' he said 'I will send it back to suppliers and see what they say!' I never heard any more and bought one from a magazine like everyone else.

I wonder where it is now and whose groin it's protecting, or did someone have it before me? Support your club!!!!

***

Dojo training excuses;

Can't come tonight I have some new shoes.
If it was in winter, I'd come.
If it was in summer, I'd come.
It's too late.
It's too early.
It's too hot.
It's too cold.
I can't lift my arms up like this so I can't do that.

My husband says it's rubbish, he used to do Judo you know.
I've just had my dinner.
I need to eat.
Must pack as I'm on holiday next week.

Excuses not given ... they usually select one from above instead of these;
Football on telly tonight,
I haven't washed my feet.
My gi is still in the wash from last week.
I did a nasty technique on that big bloke last week and I'm waiting for him to forget or take up another art.

***

67. The Yonkyo class;

It was a week long, live in, training session at the Dojo, I was there training when I could (or felt like it!) and happened to ask why we hadn't trained in yonkyo for some time. As you mostly know it's an often excruciatingly painful pressure point technique on the thumb side inner wrist .... a bit like elbowing something hard with your funny bone, that sort of feeling.
Well the teacher agreed that it was worth revisiting and planned it for the first class in the afternoon. Over lunch I had a chance to look around the garden and saw lots of jobs that really needed doing ... urgently too, I thought at the time ... so I made my excuses for missing the class.

They still did yonko ... for about an hour and a half .... as you know it is bad etiquette to scream out loud in the dojo ... unless it is a kiai of course. As I worked away on pruning and edging lawns around the dojo I could hear their silent screams passing through the walls and into outer space.
They seemed to enjoy it and all thanked me warmly of course at tea break.

68. Keeping the way.

We all, that walk this path, shall find
Sharp thorns, that seek to tear and bind.
When darkness falls, the way seems long,
But trouble not, our minds are strong.
With hearts of oak and faith that's blind
We'll find at last, this path is kind.

**

We all sit around in a ring and suppose,
but the secret sits in the middle and knows.'

Robert Frost

***

Thank you for reading this book.

Printed in Poland
by Amazon Fulfillment
Poland Sp. z o.o., Wrocław